P9-ARW-611

easy as
1-2-3
skeins™

Edited by Kara Gott Warner

HOUSE of
WHITE
BIRCHES

PUBLISHERS
SINCE 1947

Falmouth Public Library
Falmouth, MA 02540

FALMOUTH BRANCH

746.432
EAS

Easy as 1-2-3 Skeins™

EDITOR Kara Gott Warner
CREATIVE DIRECTOR Brad Snow
PUBLISHING SERVICES DIRECTOR Brenda Gallmeyer

EDITORIAL ASSISTANTS Sarah Hollman, Laurie Lehman
ASSISTANT ART DIRECTOR Nick Pierce
COPY SUPERVISOR Deborah Morgan
COPY EDITORS Emily Carter, Mary O'Donnell
TECHNICAL EDITOR Kathy Wesley
TECHNICAL ARTIST Debera Kuntz

PRODUCTION ARTIST SUPERVISOR Erin Augsburger
GRAPHIC ARTISTS Debby Keel, Amanda Treharn
PRODUCTION ASSISTANTS Marj Morgan, Judy Neuenschwander

PHOTOGRAPHY SUPERVISOR Tammy Christian
PHOTOGRAPHY Matthew Owen
PHOTO STYLISTS Tammy Liechty, Tammy Steiner

Printed in the United States of America
Library of Congress Number: 2011932398
Softcover ISBN: 978-1-59217-342-6

Easy as 1-2-3 Skeins is published by DRG, 306 East Parr Road, Berne, IN 46711.
Copyright © 2011 DRG. All rights reserved. This publication may not be
reproduced in part or in whole without written permission from the publisher.

RETAIL STORES: If you would like to carry this book or any other
DRG publications, visit DRGwholesale.com.

Every effort has been made to ensure that the instructions in this publication
are complete and accurate. We cannot, however, take responsibility for human
error, typographical mistakes or variations in individual work. Please visit
AnniesCustomerCare.com to check for pattern updates.

1 2 3 4 5 6 7 8 9

Introduction

In today's world we're all pressed for time, and like many knitters, perhaps your living space is filled to the rafters with single skeins and balls of yarn that you've been wishing you could put to good use. From the whimsical to the old standby classic, you'll find something for everyone in *Easy as 1-2-3 Skeins*. With 58 projects to choose from, you can cast on and make an adorable hat for Baby, a scarflette or a shrug. You can choose to combine a variety of skeins in various colors and textures to create that special gift.

In our Just One Skein chapter, we've got an exciting range of projects from preemie caps to stylish scarves you can make in a flash. You'll also find projects that call for multiple colors, requiring a skein of each to complete.

To stretch your stash even further, take your pick of projects from It Takes Two for imaginative ways to use two skeins or balls of yarn. All you need for the Mad for Plaid blanket are two skeins of three different-color yarns, and you've got the makings for a delightful play mat or blanket for Baby.

If garments are what you seek, Everything Good Comes in Threes gives you even more reasons to finally splurge on some luxurious yarn. You'll be thrilled to get to work on some eye-catching garments all made with just a few fabulous skeins of yarn.

Get ready to cast on some fun. It's as *Easy as 1-2-3 Skeins*!

Kara

Kara Gott Warner, editor

Hip Winter Warmers for Him & Her, page 17

Bedroom Ballet Slippers, page 37

Meanderlust, page 67

Table of Contents

. . . .

Pumpkin Seeds Vest, page 81

Ridged Moebius, page 103

Paneled Lace Afghan, page 113

Just One Skein

In this chapter, we've got everything from baby hats to single-skein scarves made in a flash. For a little excitement, we offer projects that call for multiple colors, while requiring just a skein of each to complete. If you're pressed for time, these projects will save the day as quick, gift-giving solutions. From the whimsical to the classic, you will find something for everyone.

Baby Stocking Cap

If you're looking for a last-minute gift idea, this playful topper fits the bill.

Design by Michelle Wilcox

Skill Level
■■□□ EASY

Size
Infant's size 6–12 months

Finished Measurements
Circumference: 12 inches
Height: Approx 9½ inches

Materials
- Self-striping yarn (DK weight; 100% acrylic; 147 yds/50g ber ball): 1 ball
- Size 5 (3.75mm) needles or size needed to obtain gauge
- 2½-inch-wide piece of cardboard (for tassel)

Gauge
24 sts and 30 rows = 4 inches/10cm in St st.

To save time, take time to check gauge.

Stocking Cap
Cast on 72 sts.

Work in k1, p1 rib for 1 inch.

Work even in St st until cap measures 4¾ inches, ending with a WS row.

Shape top
Row 1: [K7, k2tog] 8 times—64 sts.

Row 2: Purl across.

Rows 3–6: Work even in St st.

Row 7: [K6, k2tog] 8 times—56 sts.

Rows 8–12: Rep Rows 2–6.

Row 13: [K5, k2tog] 8 times—48 sts.

Rows 14–18: Rep Rows 2–6.

Row 19: [K4, k2tog] 8 times—40 sts.

Rows 20–24: Rep Rows 2–6.

Row 25: [K3, k2tog] 8 times—32 sts.

Rows 26–30: Rep Rows 2–6.

Row 31: [K2, k2tog] 8 times—24 sts.

Rows 32–36: Rep Rows 2–6.

Row 37: [K1, k2tog] 8 times—16 sts.

Row 38: Purl across.

Row 39: [K2tog] across—8 sts.

Cut yarn, leaving an 18-inch end.

Weave yarn through rem sts twice, pulling tightly to secure. Sew back seam.

Tassel
Wrap yarn 30 times around 2½-inch piece of cardboard. With length of yarn, tie loops tightly at 1 end. Cut other end.

With another length of yarn, wrap and tie tassel again, about ¾ inch below first tie. Attach tassel to top of cap. ●

English Popover Mittens

Chunky cables and bobbles accent these special-occasion mittens.

Design by Diane Zangl

. . . .

Skill Level

■■■□ INTERMEDIATE

Sizes

Woman's small/medium (medium/large) Instructions are given for smaller size, with larger size in parentheses. When only 1 number is given, it applies to both sizes.

Finished Measurements

Circumference: 6¾ (7¾) inches
Length: 9 (10) inches

Materials

- Brown Sheep Lamb's Pride (bulky weight; 85% wool/15% mohair; 125 yds/100g per skein): 1 (2) skein(s) wild violet #M173
- Size 6 (4mm) double-point needles (set of 4) or size needed to obtain gauge
- Cable needle
- Stitch holders
- Stitch markers

Gauge

16 sts and 24 rnds = 4 inches/10cm in St st.

To save time, take time to check gauge.

Special Abbreviations

N1, N2, N3: Needle 1, Needle 2, Needle 3.

Make 1 Left (M1L): Insert LH needle from front to back under strand between the last st worked and the next st on LH needle, k1-tbl. St slants to the left.

Make 1 Right (M1R): Insert LH needle from back to front under strand between the last st worked and the next st on LH needle, k1 through front of loop. St slants to the right.

Make Bobble (MB): (K1, yo, k1, yo, k1) all in same st, turn; p5, turn; pass 2nd, 3rd, 4th and 5th st over first, k1-tbl.

Cable over 4 back (C4B): Slip next 2 sts to cn and hold in back, k2, k2 from cn.

Cable over 4 front (C4F): Slip next 2 sts to cn and hold in front, k2, k2 from cn.

Pattern Stitches

Note: A chart is provided for those preferring to work Popover Cable pat from a chart.

Popover Cable (panel of 11 sts)
Rnd 1: P1, k9, p1.
Rnds 2, 4, 6 and 8: P1, k9, p1.
Rnd 3: P1, C4B, k1, C4F, p1.
Rnd 5: P1, k4, MB, k4, p1.
Rnd 7: P1, k3, MB, k1, MB, k3, p1.
Rep Rnds 1–8 for pat.

Mock Cable (multiple of 3 sts)
Rnd 1: *K2, p1; rep from * around.
Rnd 2: *Knit 2nd st on LH needle through front loop, leaving st on needle, knit first st, slip both sts off needle, p1; rep from * around.
Rep Rnds 1 and 2 for pat.

Left Mitten

Cuff

Cast on 27 (30) sts. Distribute sts evenly on 3 needles. Place marker for beg of rnd and join, taking care not to twist sts.

Work in Mock Cable pat until cuff measures 2½ inches, inc 2 (3) sts on last rnd—29 (33) sts.

Thumb gusset

Set up pat: K2, place marker, k1, place marker, k3, work Rnd 1 of Popover Cable pat over next 11 sts, knit to end of rnd.

Inc rnd: K2, slip marker, M1L, k1, M1R, slip marker, work in established pat to end of rnd—31 (35) sts.

Continue in established pat, inc 2 sts between markers [every other rnd] 4 (5) more times— 39 (45) sts.

Hand

K2, sl 11 (13) sts between markers to holder for thumb, cast on 1, work to end of rnd—29 (33) sts.

Work even in established pat until mitten measures 8 (9) inches from cast-on edge.

Shape top

Rnd 1: [K2tog, k1] 9 (11) times, [k2tog] 1 (0) time(s)—19 (22) sts.

Rnd 2: Knit around.

Rnd 3: K1, *k2tog, k1; rep from * around—13 (15) sts.

Rnd 4: Knit around.

Rnd 5: [K2tog] 6 (7) times, k1—7 (8) sts.

Cut yarn and draw through rem sts.

Thumb

Slip sts from holder to 2 needles, pick up and k1 in cast-on edge of opening—12 (14) sts.

Distribute sts with 4 (5) sts on N1, 4 sts on N2 and 4 (5) sts on N3. Place marker for beg of rnd and join.

Work even in St st until thumb measures 2¼ (2¾) inches.

Shape thumb top

Dec rnd: [K2tog] around—6 (7) sts.

Cut yarn and draw through rem sts.

Right Mitten

Cuff

Work same as for left cuff.

Thumb gusset

Set-up rnd: K12 (16), work Rnd 1 of Popover Cable pat over next 11 sts, k3, place marker, k1, place marker, k2.

Inc rnd: Work in established pat to last 3 sts, slip marker, M1L, k1, M1R, slip marker, k2—31 (35) sts.

Continue in established pat, inc 2 sts between markers [every other rnd] 4 (5) more times—39 (45) sts.

Hand

Work 26 (30) sts as established, sl 11 (13) sts between markers to holder for thumb, cast on 1, k2—29 (33) sts.

Work remainder of mitten same as for left mitten. ●

STITCH KEY

□	Knit
−	Purl
☐●	Bobble
	C4B
	C4F

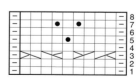

POPOVER CABLE CHART

Preemie Beanie

Just three colors of soft cotton yarn is perfect for the new arrival.

Design by Barbara Selesnick

Skill Level

◼◼◼◻ INTERMEDIATE

Size

Infant's small/27–31 weeks (medium/31–34 weeks, large/34–36 weeks) Instructions are given for smallest size, with larger sizes in parentheses. When only 1 number is given, it applies to all sizes.

Finished Measurement

Circumference: 10 (10¾, 11¼) inches

Materials

- Light weight yarn (100% cotton; 135 yds/50g per ball): 1 ball each blue, yellow, pink and orange
- Size 3 (3.25mm) double-point needles
- Size 5 (3.75mm) double-point needles or size needed to obtain gauge

Gauge

24 sts and 32 rows = 4 inches/10cm in St st with larger needles.

To save time, take time to check gauge.

Pattern Note

One ball of each color is sufficient to make several hats. Sample projects were made by alternating these colors as A, B and C.

Beanie

With smaller needles and A, cast on 56 (60, 60) sts.

Divide sts onto 3 needles and join without twisting.

Rnd 1: *K1, p1; rep from * around.

Rnds 2 and 3: Rep Rnd 1.

Change to larger needles and B.

Next rnd: Knit, inc 4 (4, 8) sts evenly around—60 (64, 68) sts.

Knit 2 rnds.

Knit 3 rnds C, 3 rnds A, 3 rnds B and 3 rnds C.

With A, knit until beanie measures 2¾ (3, 3¼) inches from beg.

Sizes small (large): Knit, dec 4 sts evenly—56 (64) sts.

Sizes medium (large): *K6, k2tog; rep from * around—56 (56) sts.

Next rnd: Knit around.

Shape top

Rnd 1: *K5, k2tog; rep from * around—48 sts.

Rnds 2, 4, 6, 8 and 10: Knit around.

Rnd 3: *K4, k2tog; rep from * around—40 sts.

Rnd 5: *K3, k2tog; rep from * around—32 sts.

Rnd 7: *K2, k2tog; rep from * around—24 sts.

Rnd 9: *K1, k2tog; rep from * around—16 sts.

Rnd 11: *K2tog; rep from * around—8 sts.

Weave yarn through rem sts and pull tight. Fasten off securely. ●

Green With Envy Scarf

Mix and match four colors of your choice with this easy first scarf project.

Design by Cynthia Adams

Skill Level
■□□□ BEGINNER

Finished Size
Approx 5 x 60 inches, excluding fringe

Materials
- Worsted weight yarn: 335 yds each dark thyme (A) and celery (B)
- Bulky weight novelty yarn: 90 yds grass green (C)
- Bulky weight novelty yarn: 70 yds mallard (D)
- Size 10½ (6.5mm) 24-inch long circular needle

[4] MEDIUM

[5] BULKY

Gauge
10 sts = 4 inches (10cm) with worsted-weight yarn.

To save time, take time to check gauge.

Special Abbreviation
Knit Wrapping Twice (KW2): Knit next st, wrapping yarn twice around needle. On next row, drop extra wrap.

Pattern Notes
Scarf is worked lengthwise; leave an 8-inch tail at each end when attaching yarns to be included in fringe.

Circular needle is used to accommodate sts; do not join. Work back and forth in rows.

Scarf
With A, cast on 110 sts.

Rows 1–4: Knit across.

Rows 5 and 6: With D, knit across.

Row 7: With B, K1, *KW2; rep from * to last st, k1.

Row 8: Knit each st, dropping 2nd wrap of each st.

Rows 9 and 10: With A, knit across.

Rows 11–14: With C, knit across.

Rows 15 and 16: With A, knit across.

Rows 17–19: With D, knit across.

Slide sts to other end of needle.

Rows 20–24: With B, knit across.

Slide sts to other end of needle.

Row 25: With C, K1, *KW2; rep from * to last st, end k1.

Row 26: Knit each st, dropping 2nd wrap of each st.

Rows 27 and 28: With A, knit across.

Fringe
Cut 15-inch strands of all yarns. Use 2 strands of assorted yarns and yarn ends for each knot.

Tie evenly spaced across each short end. ●

Hip Winter Warmers for Him & Her

Keep the happy couple snuggly warm wearing these practical and easy-to-wear warmers.

Designs by Elizabeth Decker

. . . .

Skill Level

■■■▢ INTERMEDIATE

Finished Sizes
Hats: 1 size fits most
Scarf: Approx 6 x 60 inches
Gauntlets: Small (large) Instructions are given for smaller size, with larger size in parentheses. When only 1 number is given, it applies to both sizes.

Materials
- Bulky weight yarn (100% wool): 100 yds each burnt red (A) and green (B)
- Bulky weight yarn (100% wool): 138 yds brown (C)
- Size 7 (4.5mm) double-point needles
- Size 9 (5.5mm) double-point and 16-inch circular needles or size needed to obtain gauge
- Size 11 (8mm) needles
- Stitch markers
- Stitch holders

Gauge
16 sts and 20 rnds = 4 inches/10cm in St st with size 9 needles.

To save time, take time to check gauge.

Special Abbreviations
Increase (inc): Inc 1 by knitting in front and back of st.

N1, N2, N3, N4: Needle 1, Needle 2, Needle 3, Needle 4.

Slip marker (sm): Slip marker from LH needle to RH needle.

Woman's Hat

With circular needle and C, cast on 80 sts; place marker on needle and join without twisting.

Rnds 1–5: Knit around.

Rnds 6–13: Purl around. Cut C.

Rnds 14–19: With A, *k1, p1; rep from * around. Cut A.

Rnds 20–27: With C, purl around. Cut C.

Rnds 28–47: With A, knit around.

Shape top
Rnd 1: [K6, k2tog] 10 times—70 sts.

Rnd 2 and all even-numbered rnds: Knit around.

Rnd 3: [K5, k2tog] 10 times—60 sts.

Rnd 5: [K4, k2tog] 10 times—50 sts.

Rnd 7: [K3, k2tog] 10 times—40 sts.

Rnd 9: [K2, k2tog] 10 times—30 sts.

Rnd 11: [K1, k2tog] 10 times—20 sts.

Rnd 13: [K2tog] around—10 sts.

Cut yarn, leaving a 6-inch end. Weave end through rem sts, pull tight and fasten off securely.

Scarf

Using size 11 needles and C, cast on 18 sts. Knit 2 rows, then work 4 rows in rev St st (purl on RS, knit on WS).

Working in St st, work 20 rows A, *4 rows C, [8 rows A, 2 rows C] twice, 8 rows A, 4 rows C; rep from * 4 times more.

Continuing in St st work 20 rows A.

Change to C, work 4 rows rev St st, then knit 2 rows. Bind off all sts kwise.

Gauntlets

Cuff

Using size 7 dpns and C, cast on 28 (32) sts divided as follows: N1: 9 (11) sts, N2: 9 (11) sts, N3: 10 sts. Place marker for beg of rnd and join without twisting.

Knit 2 rnds, purl 2 rnds.

Change to A and work in k1, p1 rib until cuff measures 3½ (4) inches.

Change to size 9 dpn and knit 1 rnd, inc 5 sts evenly—33 (37) sts.

Knit 4 rnds.

Thumb gusset

Rnd 1: K15 (17), place marker, k3, place marker, k15 (17).

Rnd 2: K15 (17), sm, inc 1, k1, inc 1, sm, k15 (17).

Rnds 3, 5 and 7: Knit around.

Rnd 4: K15 (17), sm, inc 1, k3, inc 1, sm, k15 (17).

Rnd 6: K15 (17), sm, inc 1, k5, inc 1, sm, k15 (17).

Rnd 8: K15 (17), sm, inc 1, k7, inc 1, sm, k15 (17)—11 sts between markers.

Rnds 9 and 10: Knit around.

Rnd 11: K15 (17), sl 11 sts between markers to a holder for thumb, cast on 3 sts, k15 (17).

Rnds 12–16: Knit around. Cut A.

Rnd 17: With C, knit around.

Rnds 18 and 19: Purl around.

Bind off all sts kwise.

Thumb

With A, pick up and knit 3 (5) sts across bound-off sts, knit across sts from holder—14 (16) sts.

Rnds 1–3: Knit around. Cut A.

Rnds 4 and 5: With C, purl around.

Bind off all sts kwise.

Man's Hat

With B and size 9 circular needle, cast on 96 sts.

Rnds 1–4: Knit around. Cut B.

Rnds 5–9: With C, *k2, p2; rep from * around. Cut C.

With B, continue in established k2, p2 rib until hat measures 5 inches from cast-on edge. Cut B.

With C, work 5 rnds k2, p2 rib. Cut C.

Shape top

Note: Change to dpns as necessary when sts no longer fit on circular needle.

Rnd 1: With B, *k2, p2, k2, ssk; rep from * around—84 sts.

Rnd 2 and all even-numbered rnds: Knit the knit sts and purl the purl sts.

Rnd 3: *K2, p2, k1, ssk; rep from * around—72 sts.

Rnd 5: *K2, p2, ssk; rep from * around—60 sts.

Rnd 7: *K2, p1, ssk; rep from * around—48 sts.

Rnd 9: *K2, ssk; rep from * around—36 sts.

Rnd 11: *K1, ssk; rep from * around—24 sts.

Rnd 13: [Ssk] around—12 sts.

Rnd 15: [Ssk] around—6 sts.

Cut yarn, leaving a 6-inch end. Weave end through rem sts, pull tight and fasten off securely. ●

Ballet Leggings

Cast on your first seamless project with these cuddly leg warmers for baby.

Design by Scarlet Taylor

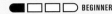

Skill Level
■□□□ BEGINNER

Size
Infant's size 6–12 months

Finished Measurements
Circumference at ankle: 6½ inches
Circumference at knee: 8½ inches
Length: 7½ inches

Materials
- DK weight yarn (100% acrylic):
  450 yds each pink (A) and pastel pink (B)
- Size 4 (3.5mm) knitting needles
- Size 5 (3.75mm) knitting needles or
  size needed to obtain gauge

3 LIGHT

Gauge
24 sts and 32 rows = 4 inches/10cm in St st with larger needles.

To save time, take time to check gauge.

Special Abbreviation
Increase (inc): Inc by making a backward loop on RH needle.

Pattern Stitch
1/1 Rib (odd number of sts)
Row 1 (RS): K1, *p1, k1; rep from * across.
Row 2: P1, *k1, p1; rep from * across.
Rep Rows 1 and 2 for pat.

Leggings
With larger needles and B, loosely cast on 39 sts.

Change to A, and work in 1/1 Rib for approx ½ inch, ending with a WS row.

Next row (RS): Work in St st, inc each end [every 4th row] once, [every 6th row] twice, [every 8th row] twice, then [every 10th row] once—51 sts.

Work even until legging measures approx 7½ inches from beg, ending with a WS row.

Change to smaller needles.

Work in 1/1 Rib for approx ½ inch, ending with a WS row.

Change to B and bind off loosely in rib.

Finishing
Sew leg seam. ●

Ballet Slippers

These easy slippers make the perfect quick-to-knit shower gift for the new baby.

Design by Scarlet Taylor

Skill Level
■■□□ EASY

Sizes
Infant's size 3–6 (6–12) months Instructions are given for smaller size, with larger size in parentheses. When only 1 number is given, it applies to both sizes.

Finished Measurement
Sole: 3¾ (4¼) inches

Materials
• DK weight yarn (100% acrylic): 450 yds pink
• Size 3 (3.25mm) knitting needles
• Size 4 (3.5mm) knitting needles
• Size 5 (3.75mm) knitting needles or size needed to obtain gauge
• 1 yd ribbon

Gauge
24 sts and 32 rows = 4 inches/10cm in St st with size 5 needles.

To save time, take time to check gauge.

Special Abbreviation
Increase (inc): Inc by knitting in front and back of next st.

Slippers

Sole
With size 5 needles, cast on 15 (18) sts.

Work in St st, inc 1 st at each end [every row] 3 times, then [every other row] once—23 (26) sts.

Work 3 (5) rows even.

Dec row (RS): K2tog, work in pat to last 2 sts, k2tog—21 (24) sts.

Continuing in St st, rep Dec row [every RS row] once, then [every row] twice—15 (18) sts.

Bind off.

Top of foot

With size 5 needles, and RS facing, pick up and knit 3 (5) sts across 1 short end of sole for toe.

Row 1 and all odd-numbered rows (WS): Purl across.

Row 2 (RS): K1 st, [inc] 2 (3) times, k0 (1) st(s)—5 (8) sts.

Row 4: K1 (2) st(s), [inc] 3 (4) times, k1 (2) st(s)—8, (12) sts.

Row 6: K2 (4) sts, [inc] 5 (5) times, k1 (3) st(s)—13, (17) sts.

Row 8: K4 (6) sts, [inc] 6 (6) times, k3 (5) sts—19 (23) sts.

Row 9: Purl across.

Row 10: Knit across.

Row 11: Purl across.

Rep [Rows 10 and 11] 6 times.

Next row (RS): K8 (10) sts, bind off center 3 sts, work across rem sts.

Working on last 8 (10) sts only, purl 1 row even.

Dec row (RS): K1, ssk, k5 (7)—7 (9) sts.

Rep Dec row [every RS row] twice—5 (7) sts.

Work 9 (11) rows even.

Bind off.

With WS facing, join yarn to rem 8 (10) sts, and purl 1 row even.

Dec row (RS): Knit to last 3 sts, k2tog, k1—7 (9) sts.

Rep Dec row [every RS row] twice—5 (7) sts.

Work 9 (13) rows even.

Bind off.

Picot cuff

With size 4 needles and RS facing, pick up and knit 30 sts around ankle edge. Beg with purl row, work 3 rows in St st.

Ribbon eyelet row (RS): K5, [k2tog, yo, k4] 3 times, k2tog, yo, k5.

Continue even in St st until cuff measures approx 1 inch, ending with a WS row.

Picot turning ridge: K1, *yo, k2tog; rep from * across, ending k1.

Change to size 3 needles and continue even in St st for approx 1 inch, ending with a WS row.

Bind off loosely.

Finishing

Sew heel seam. Sew sides of slipper and sole tog, easing in any fullness at toe.

Fold cuff hem inside at picot turning ridge, pin and sew in place.

Cut ribbon into 2 (18-inch) lengths. Weave 1 length through eyelet row of each bootie and tie bow. ●

Dressy Baby Cardigan

Every day will be a special occasion when baby wears this charming cardigan.

Design by George Shaheen

Skill Level
●●●□ INTERMEDIATE

Sizes
Infant's size 6 months (12–18 months)
Instructions are the same for both sizes;
size is determined by size of needle.

Finished Measurement
Chest: 21½ (24½) inches

Materials
- Red Heart Fiesta (worsted weight; 73% acrylic/27% nylon; 316 yds/170g per skein): 1 skein country blue #6382
- **For 6-month size:** Size 8 (5mm) circular needle or size needed to obtain gauge
- **For 12–18-month size:** Size 9 (5.5mm) circular needle or size needed to obtain gauge
- 4 stitch holders
- 3 (½-inch) white buttons
- Sewing needle and matching thread

Gauge
For 6-month size: 17 sts and 24 rows = 4 inches in St st on smaller needle.

For 12–18-month size: 15 sts and 20 rows = 4 inches in St st on larger needle.

To save time, take time to check gauge.

Pattern Notes
Circular needle is used to accommodate large number of stitches in yoke. Do not join; work back and forth in rows.

Slip all stitches purlwise.

Special Abbreviation
Increase (inc): Inc by knitting in front and back of next st.

Back
Cast on 51 sts.

Row 1 (WS): Purl across.

Row 2 (RS): K2, [yo, k2, sl 1, k2tog, psso, k2, yo, k1] 6 times, k1.

Row 3: Purl across.

Rows 4–29: [Rep Rows 2 and 3] 13 times.

Armhole shaping
Row 1 (RS): Bind off 3 sts, sl 1, k2tog, psso, k2, yo, k1, [yo, k2, sl 1, k2tog, psso, k2, yo, k1] 4 times, yo, k2, sl 1, k2tog, psso, k4—46 sts.

Row 2: Bind off 3 sts, purl across—43 sts.

Row 3: K1, k2tog, k5, [sl 1, k2tog, psso, k5] 4 times, sl 1, k1, psso, k1—33 sts.

Row 4: Purl across.

Slip rem sts onto holder for back yoke, cut yarn.

Sleeves
Cast on 35 sts.

Row 1 (WS): Purl across.

Row 2 (RS): K2, [yo, k2, sl 1, k2tog, psso, k2, yo, k1] 4 times, k1.

Row 3 and all WS rows: Purl across.

Row 4: Inc, k1, [yo, k2, sl 1, k2tog, psso, k2, yo, k1] 4 times, inc—37 sts.

Row 6: K3, [yo, k2, sl 1, k2tog, psso, k2, yo, k1] 4 times, k2.

Row 8: Inc, k2, [yo, k2, sl 1, k2tog, psso, k2, yo, k1] 4 times, k1, inc—39 sts.

Row 10: K4, [yo, k2, sl 1, k2tog, psso, k2, yo, k1] 4 times, k3.

Row 12: Inc, k3, [yo, k2, sl 1, k2tog, psso, k2, yo, k1] 4 times, k2, inc—41 sts.

Row 14: K5, [yo, k2, sl 1, k2tog, psso, k2, yo, k1] 4 times, k4.

Row 16: Inc, k4, [yo, k2, sl 1, k2tog, psso, k2, yo, k1] 4 times, k3, inc—43 sts.

Row 18: K6, [yo, k2, sl 1, k2tog, psso, k2, yo, k1] 4 times, k5.

Row 20: Inc, k5, [yo, k2, sl 1, k2tog, psso, k2, yo, k1] 4 times, k4, inc—45 sts.

Row 22: K7, [yo, k2, sl 1, k2tog, psso, k2, yo, k1] 4 times, k6.

Row 24: Inc, k6, [yo, k2, sl 1, k2tog, psso, k2, yo, k1] 4 times, k5, inc—47 sts.

Row 26: K8, [yo, k2, sl 1, k2tog, psso, k2, yo, k1] 4 times, k7.

Row 27: Purl across.

Rows 28–33: Rep [Rows 26 and 27] 3 times.

Armhole shaping
Row 1 (RS): Bind off 3 sts, k4, [yo, k2, sl 1, k2tog, psso, k2, yo, k1] 4 times, k7—44 sts.

Row 2: Bind off 3 sts, purl across—41 sts.

Row 3: K1, k2tog, k4, [sl 1, k2tog, psso, k5] 3 times, sl 1, k2tog, psso, k4, sl 1, k1, psso, k1—31 sts.

Row 4: Purl across.

Slip rem sts onto holder for sleeve yoke, cut yarn.

Left Front
Cast on 29 sts.

Row 1 (WS): Purl across.

Row 2 (RS): K2, [yo, k2, sl 1, k2tog, psso, k2, yo, k1] 3 times, p3.

Row 3: K3, purl to end.

Row 4: K2, [yo, k2, sl 1, k2tog, psso, k2, yo, k1] 3 times, k3.

Row 5: Purl across.

Rows 6–29: Rep [Rows 2–5] 6 times.

Armhole shaping
Row 1 (RS): Bind off 3 sts, sl 1, k2tog, psso, k2, yo, k1, [yo, k2, sl 1, k2tog, psso, k2, yo, k1] twice, p3—25 sts.

Row 2: K3, purl to end.

Row 3: K1, k2tog, k5, [sl 1, k2tog, psso, k5] twice, k1—20 sts.

Row 4: Purl across.

Slip rem sts onto holder for sleeve yoke, cut yarn.

Right Front
Cast on 29 sts.

Row 1 (WS): Purl across.

Row 2 (RS): P3, k1, [yo, k2, sl 1, k2tog, psso, k2, yo, k1] 3 times, k1.

Row 3: Purl to last 3 sts, k3.

Row 4: K4, [yo, k2, sl 1, k2tog, psso, k2, yo, k1] 3 times, k1.

Row 5: Purl across.

Rows 6–29: Rep [Rows 2–5] 6 times.

Armhole shaping
Row 1 (RS): P3, k1, [yo, k2, sl 1, k2tog, psso, k2, yo, k1] twice, yo, k2, sl 1, k2tog, psso, k4—28 sts.

Row 2: Bind off 3 sts, purl to last 3 sts, k3—25 sts.

Row 3: K6, [sl 1, k2tog, psso, k5] twice, sl 1, k1, psso, k1—20 sts.

Row 4: Purl across.

Do not cut yarn.

Yoke shaping
Row 1 (RS): With RS facing, p20 for right front, p31 from holder for 1 sleeve, p33 from holder for back, p31 from holder for 2nd sleeve, p20 from holder for left front—135 sts.

Rows 2 and 3: Knit across.

Row 4: P8, [p2tog, p11] 9 times, p2tog, p8—125 sts.

Row 5: Purl across.

Row 6: Knit across.

Row 7 (buttonhole row for boy): Knit to last 4 sts, k2tog, yo, k2.

Row 7 (buttonhole row for girl): K2, yo, k2tog, knit to end.

Row 8: P8, [p2tog, p10] 9 times, p2tog, p7—115 sts.

Row 9: Purl across.

Rows 10 and 11: Knit across.

Row 12: P7, [p2tog, p9] 9 times, p2tog, p7—105 sts.

Row 13: Purl across.

Rows 14 and 15: Knit across.

Row 16: P7, [p2tog, p8] 9 times, p2tog, p6—95 sts.

Row 17: Purl across.

Row 18: Knit across.

Row 19 (buttonhole row for boy): Knit to last 4 sts, k2tog, yo, k2.

Row 19 (buttonhole row for girl): K2, yo, k2tog, knit to end.

Row 20: P6, [p2tog, p7] 9 times, p2tog, p6—85 sts.

Row 21: Purl across.

Rows 22 and 23: Knit across.

Row 24: P6, [p2tog, p6] 9 times, p2tog, p5—75 sts.

Row 25: Purl across.

Rows 26 and 27: Knit across.

Row 28: P5, [p2tog, p5] 10 times—65 sts.

Row 29: Purl across.

Row 30: Knit across.

Row 31 (buttonhole row for boy): Knit to last 4 sts, k2tog, yo, k2.

Row 31 (buttonhole row for girl): K2, yo, k2tog, knit across.

Bind off as follows: p4, [p2tog, p4] 10 times, p1.

Finishing
Block lace pat flat.

Sew side and sleeve seams. Sew armhole seams. Sew buttons opposite buttonholes, 2 sts in from edge, making sure buttons are secure. ●

Button-Up Hat

Cast on this weekend to make this fun quick-knit hat.

Design by Julie Gaddy

Skill Level

■■■□ INTERMEDIATE

Size
Toddler's size 24 months

Finished Measurements
Circumference: 12 inches
Height: Approx 9½ inches

Materials
- Worsted weight yarn (75% acrylic/ 25% wool; 200 yds/100g per ball): 1 ball each navy blue (A), pale orange (B) and red (C)
- Size 5 (3.75mm) 16-inch circular needle
- Size 8 (5mm) double-point and 16-inch circular needles or size needed to obtain gauge
- Stitch markers
- 5 (⅞-inch) buttons: 4 red, 1 blue

Gauge
18 sts = 4 inches/10cm in St st with larger needles.

To save time, take time to check gauge.

Hat

Ribbing
With smaller needle and A, cast on 96 sts. Place marker on needle and join without twisting.

Rnds 1–6: *K1, p1; rep from * around.

Body
Rnd 1 (buttonhole rnd): [Bind off 3 sts, work in established ribbing for 21 sts] 4 times—84 sts.

Rnd 2: Work in established ribbing, casting on 3 sts over each group of bound-off sts—96 sts.

Continue in ribbing until hat measures 4 inches from beg.

Change to B and larger circular needle. Work in St st until hat measures 7 inches from beg.

Change to C and work even until hat measures 8 inches from beg.

Shape crown
Note: Change to dpns as needed.

Rnd 1: [K10, k2tog] 8 times—88 sts.

Rnd 2 and all even-numbered rnds: Knit around.

Rnd 3: [K9, k2tog] 8 times—80 sts.

Rnd 5: [K8, k2tog] 8 times—72 sts.

Rnd 7: [K7, k2tog] 8 times—64 sts.

Rnd 9: [K6, k2tog] 8 times—56 sts.

Rnd 11: [K5, k2tog] 8 times—48 sts.

Rnd 13: [K4, k2tog] 8 times—40 sts.

Rnd 15: [K3, k2tog] 8 times—32 sts.

Rnd 17: [K2, k2tog] 8 times—24 sts.

Rnd 18: [K1, k2tog] 8 times—16 sts.

Rnd 19: [K2tog] around—8 sts.

Cut yarn, leaving a 10-inch tail. Weave yarn through rem sts, pull tight and fasten off.

Finishing
Sew 4 red buttons on line between ribbing and St st portion of hat, lining buttons up with buttonholes. Sew blue button at top of hat, covering drawn-up sts. Block lightly if desired. ●

Pull-Top Beanie

Easy to make and wear, this topper is the perfect holiday gift.

Design by Edie Eckman

Skill Level
■ ■ □ □ EASY

Finished Size
Fits 22- to 23-inch circumference head

Materials
- Lion Brand Wool-Ease Chunky (chunky weight; 80% acrylic/20% wool; 153 yds/140g per ball): 1 ball each spice #135 (A) and walnut #127 (B) **5 BULKY**
- Size 10½ (6.5mm) 16-inch circular needle or size needed to obtain gauge
- Stitch marker

Gauge
13 sts and 19 rows = 4 inches/10cm in St st.

To save time, take time to check gauge.

Special Abbreviation
Make 1 (M1): Inc by inserting LH needle from front to back under horizontal thread between st just worked and next st, knit into back loop.

Beanie

Body
With A, loosely cast on 57 sts. Place marker for beg of rnd; join, being careful not to twist sts.

Rnd 1: Purl around.

Rnd 2: Knit around.

Rnd 3: Purl around.

Rnd 4: With B, k1, [M1, k11] 5 times, k1—62 sts.

Rnds 5–7: Knit around.

Rnd 8: With A, k1 [k2tog, k10] 5 times, k1—57 sts.

Rnds 9–12: Rep Rnds 1–4.

Knit every rnd until beanie measures 7 inches from beg.

Shape top
Rnd 1: With A, k1, [k2tog, k8] 6 times, k1—56 sts.

Rnd 2: Purl around.

Rnd 3: [K6, k2tog] 7 times—49 sts.

Rnd 4: Purl around.

Rnd 5: K2, [k2tog, k5] 6 times, k2tog, k3—42 sts.

Rnd 6: Purl around.

Rnd 7 (eyelet rnd): [K4, yo, k2tog] 7 times.

Rnd 8: Purl around.

Rnd 9: Knit around.

Rnd 10: Purl around.

Rnds 11 and 12: Rep Rnds 9 and 10.

Bind off.

Finishing

Twisted cord
Cut 2 strands of B, each 60 inches long. Tie ends to a door handle or hook. Twist strands counterclockwise until yarn twists up on itself when relaxed. Hold yarn at middle of twisted strand, remove end from handle and allow yarn to twist onto itself. Cut twisted cord 18 inches long. Tie overhand knot 1½ inches from each end. Thread cord through eyelets, beg and ending in same opening. Pull ends of cord to gather top and tie into a knot. ●

Mary Janes

Those little piggies will be sweet enough to eat wearing these precious booties!

Design by Scarlet Taylor

Skill Level
■□□□ EASY

Sizes
Infant's size 3–6 (6–9, 9–12) months Instructions are given for smallest size, with larger sizes in parentheses. When only 1 number is given, it applies to all sizes.

Finished Measurement
Sole: 3 (3¾, 4½) inches long

Materials
- Bernat Softee Baby yarn (DK weight; 100% acrylic; 395 yds/140g per ball): 1 ball white #02000
- Size 5 (3.75mm) needles or size needed to obtain gauge
- Stitch holder
- ¼ yard ⅜-inch-wide pink-and-white polka-dot ribbon
- 2 (½-inch diameter) buttons

3 LIGHT

Gauge
24 sts and 42 rows = 4 inches/10cm in Seed St pat.

To save time, take time to check gauge.

Pattern Stitch
Seed St (odd number of sts)
Row 1: P1, *k1, p1; rep from * across.
Rep Row 1 for pat.

Booties

Toe cap
Cast on 9 sts.

Work 12 rows even in Seed St pat.

Cut yarn.

Sides
Cast on 16 (18, 20) sts.

With RS facing, pick up and knit 8 (8, 10) sts evenly spaced along RS of toe cap, work in Seed St pat across 9 sts of toe top, pick up and knit 8 (8, 10) sts evenly spaced along left side of toe cap, cast on 16 (18, 20) sts—57 (61, 69) sts.

Continue even in Seed St pat until sides measure approx 1 inch, ending with a WS row.

Next row (RS): Bind off 24 (26, 30) sts, work in Seed St pat across next 9 sts (including st left from bind-off), bind off rem 24 (26, 30) sts—9 sts.

Cut yarn.

Sole

Hold bootie with WS facing, join yarn and work even in Seed St pat on rem 9 sts until sole measures approx 3 (3¾, 4½) inches. Place sts on holder for heel. ***Note:*** *Sole should be slightly shorter than sides.*

Assembly

Sew sides of bootie, slightly stretched, to edges of sole wrapping end of sides around heel edge of sole to meet in center. Adjust length of sole if necessary and bind off sts. Join heel seam.

Strap

Left bootie

On right side of bootie, measure approx ½ (¾, ¾) inch, from cast-on edge of toe cap. Pick up and knit 3 sts for strap.

Work in Seed St pat until strap measures approx 2½ inches from beg. Bind off.

Right bootie

Work as for left bootie, picking up sts from left side of bootie.

Finishing

Attach buttons, sewing through strap and bootie. Cut ribbon in half and tie each half in bow. Referring to photo for placement, sew 1 bow to top of each bootie. •

Lacy Stripe Cardigan

This charming cardigan with lacy accents is a perfect quick-to-stitch springtime piece.

Design by Lorna Miser

Skill Level

■■■□ INTERMEDIATE

Sizes

Baby's/toddler's size 6 months (1 year, 2 years) Instructions are given for the smallest size, with larger sizes in parentheses. When only 1 number is given, it applies to all sizes.

Finished Measurement

Chest: 20 (22, 24) inches

Materials

- TLC Cotton Plus (medium weight; 51% cotton/49% acrylic; 153 yds/100g per skein): 1 skein each light blue #3810 (A), lavender #3590 (B), medium rose #3707 (C) and light rose #3706 (D)
- Size 7 (4.5mm) 29-inch circular needle or size needed to obtain gauge
- Stitch markers
- Stitch holders
- 20 inches 1-inch-wide organza ribbon
- Sewing needle and matching thread

Gauge

18 sts = 4 inches/10cm in Lace pat.

To save time, take time to check gauge.

Special Abbreviation

Increase (inc): Inc by knitting in front and back of next st.

Pattern Stitches

Lace (multiple of 2 sts)
Row 1 (RS): With new color, knit across.
Rows 2 and 3: Knit across.
Row 4: Purl across.
Row 5: K1, *yo, k2tog; rep from * to last st, k1.
Row 6: Purl across.
Rep Rows 1–6 for pat.

Stripe Sequence

Work Lace pat in following color sequence:
*6 rows A,
6 rows B,
6 rows C,
6 rows D.
Rep from * for Stripe Sequence.

Pattern Note

Body of sweater is worked in 1 piece to underarms, and then divided and shaped for fronts and back. Sleeves are knit flat and then sewn to body.

Body

With A, cast on 90 (100, 108) sts.

Next row: K4, place marker, work in Lace pat to last 4 sts, place marker, k4.

Keeping first and last 4 sts in garter st and sts between markers in Lace pat, continue in established pat working Lace pat in Stripe Sequence until body measures approximately 6 (6, 7) inches from cast-on edge, ending with a Row 2 or 6 of Lace pat.

Divide for armholes

Work in pat across 23 (25, 27) sts for right front and place sts on holder; work in pat across next 44 (50, 54) sts for back. Place rem 23 (25, 27) sts on holder for left front.

Back

Work in established pat on back sts until armhole measures 3½ (4, 4½) inches, ending with a Row 2 or 6 of Lace pat.

Neck edging

Next row: Work in pat across 11 (14, 16) sts, place marker, knit center 22 sts, place marker, work in pat across 11 (14, 16) sts.

Rep last row until armhole measures 4 (4½, 5) inches.

Bind off all sts.

Right Front
Place right front sts on needles.

Neck shaping
Note: *Work dec at neck edge 4 sts in from edge, keeping 4 sts at center front in garter st.*

Continue in pat, dec 1 st by k2tog at neck edge [every RS row] 11 times—11 (14, 16) sts.

Work even until front measures same as back to shoulders.

Bind off all sts.

Left Front
Place left front sts on needles.

Neck shaping
Note: *Work dec at neck edge 4 sts in from edge, keeping 4 sts at center front in garter st.*

Continue in pat, dec 1 st by ssk at neck edge [every RS row] 11 times—11 (14, 16) sts.

Work even until front measures same as back to shoulders.

Bind off all sts.

Sleeves
With A, cast on 22 sts.

Work in Lace pat and *at the same time* inc 1 st at each edge [every 4th row] 7 (9, 12) times, working additional sts into pat—36 (40, 46) sts.

Work even until sleeve measures 6½ (7, 8) inches.

Bind off all sts.

Finishing
Sew shoulder seams.

Sew sleeve into armhole, matching center of top of sleeve to shoulder seam.

Cut ribbon in half. Sew 1 piece to inside of each front edge just below first neck dec. ●

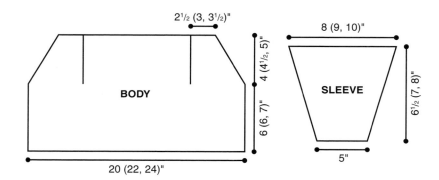

Start the school year in style with this cover for a notebook!

Design by Celeste Pinheiro

Skill Level
■■□□ EASY

Finished Size
Fits 1- and 1½-inch binders

Materials
- Plymouth Encore Worsted (worsted weight; 75% acrylic/25% wool; 200 yds/100g per ball): 1 ball each turquoise #1317 (A), bright pink #137 (B), gold #1014 (C) and salmon #457 (D)
- Size 8 (5mm) needles or size needed to obtain gauge
- Sewing needle and matching thread

Gauge
18 sts = 4 inches/10cm in St st.

To save time, take time to check gauge.

Pattern Stitch
Color Stripe (odd number of sts)
Row 1 (RS): With A, purl across.
Rows 2 and 3: With A, work in St st.
Row 4: P1 A, *p1 D, p1 A; rep from * across.
Rows 5 and 6: With A, work in St st.
Rows 7 and 8: With B, purl across.
Rows 9 and 10: With C, work in St st.
Row 11: K1 D, *k1 C, k1 D; rep from * across.
Row 12: P1 D, *p1 C, p1 D; rep from * across.
Row 13: With D, knit across.
Row 14: With A, knit across.
Rows 15–19: With A, work in St st.
Rows 20 and 21: With D, knit across.
Rows 22–24: With C, work in St st.
Row 25: K1 C, *k1 B, k1 C; rep from * across.
Row 26: With B, purl across.
Rep Rows 1–26 for pat.

Cover

Inside flap
With B cast on 51 sts. Knit 3 rows.

Work in St st until cover measures 10 inches from beg, ending with a WS row.

Body
Work [Rows 1–26 of Color Stripe pat] 4 times, then rep Rows 1–20.

Inside flap
With D, continue in St st until cover measures 9½ inches from last Row 20.

Knit 4 rows. Bind off all sts.

Finishing
Referring to photo for placement and using chain sts (see page 124), with B, embroider daisies on A stripe. With D, work French knot center (see page 125).

Sew flaps to cover at top and bottom edges. ●

No Cold Footsies

Use yarn with a little stretch for these socks that will stay put on active little feet.

Designs by Hélène Rush

Alligator Baby Socks

Skill Level

■■■□ INTERMEDIATE

Size
Infant's size 6–9 months

Finished Measurement
Length from toe to heel: Approx 3½ inches

Materials
- Knit One, Crochet Too Soxx Appeal (sock weight; 96% superwash merino wool/3% nylon/1% elastic; 208 yds/ 50g per ball): 1 ball avocado #9577
- Size 2 (2.75mm) double-point needles (set of 4) or size needed to obtain gauge
- Stitch marker
- Stitch holder

1 SUPER FINE

Squiggles Child's Socks

Skill Level

■■■□ INTERMEDIATE

Sizes
Child's small/medium (medium/large) Instructions are given for smaller size, with larger size in parentheses. When only 1 number is given, it applies to both sizes.

Materials
- Knit One, Crochet Too Soxx Appeal (sock weight; 94% superwash merino wool/3% nylon/1% elastic; 208 yds/50g per ball): 1 ball oceana #9627
- Size 2 (2.75mm) set of 4 double-point needles or size needed to obtain gauge
- Stitch holder
- Stitch marker

1 SUPER FINE

Alligator Baby Socks

Gauge
32 sts = 4 inches/10cm in St st.

To save time, take time to check gauge.

Special Abbreviations
Make 1 (M1): Inc by k1-tbl of horizontal strand between st just worked and next st on LH needle.

Slip, slip, knit (ssk): Slip next st kwise, slip next st through back loop, knit 2 slipped sts tog.

N1, N2, N3, N4: Needle 1, Needle 2, Needle 3, Needle 4.

Pattern Stitch
Alligator (multiple of 6 sts)
Rnds 1–3: *K4, p2; rep from * around.
Rnd 4: *Yo, k2tog, ssk, yo, p2; rep from * around.
Rep Rnds 1–4 for pat.

Pattern Note
Slip all stitches purlwise unless otherwise specified.

Socks

Cuff

Cast on 36 sts, placing 12 sts on each needle, place marker and join without twisting.

Ribbing

Rnds 1–14: *K2, p2; rep from * around.

Leg

Rep [Rnds 1–4 of Alligator pat] 4 times. Rep Rnd 1 once more.

Heel flap

Slip last st on last needle to first needle.

Row 1 (RS): Sl 1, k17, turn, leaving rem 18 sts on holder for instep.

Row 2: *Sl 1, p1; rep from * across.

Rep [Rows 1 and 2] 7 times more.

Turn heel

Row 1 (RS): Sl 1, k8, k2tog, k1, turn—6 sts rem unworked.

Row 2: Sl 1, p1, p2tog, p1, turn—6 sts rem unworked.

Row 3: Sl 1, k2, k2tog, k1, turn—4 sts rem unworked.

Row 4: Sl 1, p3, p2tog, p1, turn—4 sts rem unworked.

Continue in this manner until all sts are worked—10 sts.

Gusset

Rnd 1: N1: sl 1, knit across heel sts, pick up and knit 9 sts evenly along side of heel flap, M1 in strand before first st on holder for instep; N2: work across 18 sts for instep maintaining established pat; N3: M1 in strand after last st from instep, pick up and knit 9 sts evenly along side of heel flap, knit first 5 sts from heel needle (you are now at center back)—48 sts (15 sts on N1 and N3, 18 sts on N2).

Rnd 2: N1: knit to last 3 sts, k2tog, k1; N2: work even in established pat; N3: K1, ssk, knit to end of rnd—46 sts.

Rnd 3: Knit around.

Rep Rnds 2 and 3 until 36 sts rem.

Foot

Work even until foot measures ½ inch less than desired finished length.

Toe

Rnd 1: N1: knit to last 3 sts, k2tog, k1; N2: k1, ssk, knit to last 3 sts, k2tog, k1; N3: k1, ssk, knit to end of needle—32 sts rem.

Rnd 2: Knit around.

Rep Rnds 1 and 2 until 20 sts rem.

Weave toe sts tog using Kitchener st, page 122.

Squiggles Child's Socks

Gauge

32 sts = 4 inches/10cm in St st.

To save time, take time to check gauge.

Special Abbreviations

Make 1 (M1): Inc by k1-tbl of horizontal strand between st just worked and next st on LH needle.

Slip, slip, knit (ssk): Slip next st kwise, slip next st through back loop, knit 2 slipped sts tog.

N1, N2, N3, N4: Needle 1, Needle 2, Needle 3, Needle 4.

Pattern Stitch
Squiggles (multiple of 18 (20) sts)
Rnd 1: Purl around.
Rnds 2 and 3: Knit around.
Rnd 4: *K1 (3), [k2tog] 3 times, [yo, k1] 5 times, yo, [k2tog] 3 times; rep from * across each needle.
Rnds 5 and 6: Knit around.
Rep Rnds 1–6 for pat.

Pattern Notes
One ball of yarn is enough to make the largest size with a 5-inch-long foot. For longer socks, purchase additional ball of yarn.

Slip all stitches purlwise unless specified otherwise.

Socks

Cuff
Cast on 42 (48) sts, placing 14 (16) sts on each needle. Mark beg of rnd and join without twisting.

Ribbing
Rnd 1: *K2, p2; rep from * around.

Rnds 2–12: Rep Rnd 1.

Rnd 13: Rep Rnd 1, inc 4 sts evenly across each needle—54 (60) sts.

Leg
Work even in Squiggles pat until sock measures approx 3 (3½) inches from beg, ending with Rnd 1 and dec 12 sts evenly in last rnd—42 (48) sts.

Heel flap
Row 1 (RS): Sl 1, k20 (23), turn, leaving rem 21 (24) sts on holder for instep.

Row 2: *Sl 1, p1; rep from * across.

Rep Rows 1 and 2 for a total of 24 (28) rows.

Turn heel
Row 1 (RS): Sl 1, k11 (12), k2tog, k1, turn—6 (8) sts rem unworked.

Row 2: Sl 1, p4 (3), p2tog, p1, turn—6 (8) sts rem unworked.

Row 3: Sl 1, k5 (4), k2tog, k1, turn—4 (6) sts rem unworked.

Row 4: Sl 1, p6 (5), p2tog, p1, turn—4 (6) sts rem unworked.

Continue to work in this manner until all sts are worked—13 (14) sts rem.

Gusset
Rnd 1: N1: sl 1, knit across heel sts, dec 1 (0) st(s) at center of row (12 (14) heel sts rem), working on side of heel, with same needle, pick up and knit 11 (13) sts evenly along side of heel flap, M1 in strand before first st on holder for instep; N2: knit across 21 (24) sts for instep; N3: M1 in strand after last st from instep, pick up and knit 11 (13) sts evenly along side of heel flap, knit first 6 (7) sts from heel needle (you are now at center back of sock)—57 (66) sts (18 (21) sts on N1 and N3, and 21 (24) sts on N2).

Rnd 2: N1: knit to last 3 sts, k2tog, k1; N2: knit across; N3: k1, ssk, knit to end of rnd—55 (64) sts.

Rnd 3: Knit around.

Rep Rnds 2 and 3 until 42 (48) sts rem.

Foot
Work even until foot measures 1 inch less than desired finished length.

Note: Distribute sts as follows: N2: 21 (24) sts and 21 (24) sts divided between N1 and N2.

Toe
Rnd 1: N1: knit to last 3 sts, k2tog, k1; N2: k1, ssk, knit to last 3 sts, k2tog, k1; N3: k1, ssk, knit to end of needle—32 sts.

Rnd 2: Knit around.

Rep Rnds 1 and 2 until 18 (24) sts rem.

Weave toe sts tog using Kitchener st, page 122. ●

Bedroom Ballet Slippers

Release her inner ballerina and keep her on her toes with these oh-so-simple slippers.

Design by DROPS Design for Garnstudio

Skill Level

◼◼◻◻ EASY

Sizes

Woman's shoe size 5–6½ (7½–9, 9½–10½) Instructions are given for smallest size, with larger sizes in parentheses. When only 1 number is given, it applies to all sizes.

Finished Measurement

Foot length: 8¾ (9½, 10½) inches

Materials

- Garnstudio DROPS Alpaca (sport weight; 100% alpaca; 182 yds/50g per skein): 1 skein teal #2919
- Size 3 (3.25mm) needles or size needed to obtain gauge
- Stitch holder
- Stitch marker

2 FINE

Gauge

24 sts and 32 rows = 4 inches/10cm in k2, p2 pat.

To save time, take time to check gauge.

Special Abbreviation

Increase (inc): Inc by purling in front and then back of next st.

Slippers

Strap

Cast on 8 (8, 9) sts.

Work in garter st for 3 (3, 3½) inches. Cut yarn and slip sts onto holder.

Foot

Cast on 18 (20, 23) sts, knit across sts on holder, cast on 15 (16, 18) sts—41 (44, 50) sts.

Knit 5 rows (mark first row as WS).

Inc row (RS): K1 (edge st), k1, [inc, k2] 12 (13, 15) times, inc, k1, end k1 (edge st)—54 (58, 66) sts.

Next row (WS): K1, p1, k2, *p2, k2; rep from * to last 2 sts, p1, k1.

Next row (RS): K2, *p2, k2; rep from * across.

Rep last 2 rows until slipper measures 6¼ (6¾, 7) inches from foot cast-on, ending with a WS row.

Dec row (RS): K2, *p2tog, k2; rep from * across—41 (44, 50) sts.

Knit 5 rows.

Bind off loosely.

Assembly

Fold foot in half with WS of cast-on and bound-off edges tog. Sew ends of rows tog to form heel and toe.

Sew strap to opposite side of slipper. ●

Undulations Socks

Use a fingering-weight yarn for these easy-to-make, perfect-fit socks for any size!

Design by Amy Polcyn

Skill Level

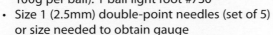 ■■■□ INTERMEDIATE

Sizes

Woman's small (medium, large, extra-large) to fit shoe sizes 6/6½ (7/7½, 8/8½, 9/9½) Instructions are given for smallest size, with larger sizes in parentheses. When only 1 number is given, it applies to all sizes. When 2 numbers are given, the smaller is for a narrow/medium foot and the larger is for a wider foot.

Finished Measurements

Length: 8¾ (9, 9¼, 9¾) inches
Circumference: 8 (9½) inches

Materials

- SWTC TOFUtsies (sock weight; 50% superwash wool/25% soysilk/ 22.5% cotton/2.5% chitin; 465 yds/ 100g per ball): 1 ball light foot #730
- Size 1 (2.5mm) double-point needles (set of 5) or size needed to obtain gauge
- Small crochet hook
- Spare needle 1 or 2 sizes larger
- Stitch marker

Gauge

30 sts and 46 rows = 4 inches/10cm in St st.

To save time, take time to check gauge.

Special Abbreviations

N1, N2, N3, N4: Needle 1, Needle 2, Needle 3, Needle 4.

Wrap and Turn (W/T): Move yarn between needles to RS, slip next st, move yarn back to WS, turn piece, slip st back to other needle.

Special Technique

Provisional Cast-On: With crochet hook and waste yarn, make a chain several sts longer than desired cast-on. With knitting needle and project yarn, pick up and knit indicated number of sts in "bumps" on back of chain. When indicated in pat, "unzip" crochet chain to free live sts.

Pattern Stitch

Note: A chart is provided for those preferring to work Undulation pat from a chart.

Undulation (multiple of 6 sts)
Rnds 1 and 2: *P4, k2; rep from * to end.
Rnds 3 and 4: *P3, k3; rep from * to end.
Rnds 5 and 6: *P2, k4; rep from * to end.
Rnds 7 and 8: *P1, k4, p1; rep from * to end.
Rnds 9 and 10: *P1, k3, p2; rep from * to end.
Rnds 11 and 12: *P1, k2, p3; rep from * to end.
Rep Rnds 1–12 for pat.

Pattern Notes

Work length appropriate for shoe size. Smaller stitch count is for narrow/medium width foot; larger stitch count is for wider foot.

Sock circumference should be approximately 10 percent less than actual foot measurement allowing for "negative ease" and a snug, non-slouchy fit.

To ensure a very loose bind-off, use needle size 1 or 2 sizes larger to bind off.

Needles 1 and 4 hold the sole stitches; Needles 2 and 3 hold the instep stitches.

Socks

Using Provisional Cast-On method and single dpn, cast on 30 (36) sts.

Purl 1 row.

Short-row toe

Row 1 (RS): Knit to last st, W/T.

Row 2: Purl to last st, W/T.

Row 3: Knit to st before last wrapped st, W/T.

Row 4: Purl to st before last wrapped st, WT.

Rep Rows 3 and 4 until 9 (10) sts are wrapped on each side, leaving 12 (16) sts unworked in center of row. Half of the toe is complete.

Next row (RS): Knit to first wrapped st, knit st tog with wrap, W/T.

Note: Next st will now have 2 wraps. On subsequent rows, knit wrapped st tog with both wraps.

Next row: Purl to first wrapped st, purl st tog with wrap, wrap and turn.

Note: Next st will now have 2 wraps. On subsequent rows, knit wrapped st tog with both wraps.

Rep last 2 rows until all sts have been worked and no wraps rem. Toe is complete.

Foot

Set-up rnd: N4: k15 (18), place marker for beg of rnd; N1: k15 (18); carefully unzip the Provisional Cast-On st by st and sl 15 (18) sts each to N2 and N3; pick up a running thread between N1 and N2, and with N1, k1-tbl; N2 and N3: knit; N4: pick up a running thread between N3 and N4 and k1-tbl, knit to end—62 (74) sts.

Rnd 1: N1: knit to last 2 sts, k2tog; N2 and N3: work in pat; N4: ssk, knit to end—60 (72) sts.

Continue working in St st on N1 and N4, and Undulation pat on N2 and N3 until sock measures 7 (7¼, 7½, 8) inches or approx 1¾ inches less than desired length, ending with N3.

Short-row heel

Slip sts on N4 and N1 to 1 dpn for heel, keeping sts on N2 and N3 on hold.

Work short-row heel as for short-row toe.

Leg

Work in rnds, working Undulation pat on all sts until leg measures 6 inches or desired length.

Work in k2, p2 rib for 1 inch.

Bind off very loosely in rib.

Finishing

Weave in ends, block if desired. ●

STITCH KEY
☐ Knit
⊟ Purl

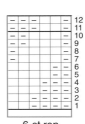

6-st rep
UNDULATION CHART

Nautical Striped Booties

The little newcomer will make an impression wearing these treats for the feet.

Design by Scarlet Taylor

Skill Level

■■■□ INTERMEDIATE

Sizes
Infant's size 3–6 (6–9, 9-12) months Instructions are given for smallest size, with larger sizes in parentheses. When only 1 number is given, it applies to all sizes.

Finished Measurement
Sole: 3 (3¾, 4½) inches long

Materials
- TLC Cotton Plus (worsted weight; 51% cotton/49% acrylic; 153 yds/100g per skein): 1 skein each navy #3859 (A), medium blue #3811 (B) and white #3001 (C)
- Size 5 (3.75mm) needles
- Size 6 (4mm) needles or size needed to obtain gauge

4 MEDIUM

Gauge
22 sts and 30 rows = 4 inches/10cm in St st with larger needles.

To save time, take time to check gauge.

Special Abbreviation
Increase (inc): Inc by knitting in front and back of next st.

Pattern Stitches
Stripe
Work following stripe sequence in St st:
2 rows C,
2 rows B,
2 rows A.

1/1 Rib (odd number of sts)
Row 1: K1, *p1, k1; rep from * across.
Row 2: P1, *k1, p1; rep from * across.
Rep Rows 1 and 2 for pat.

Booties

Sole
With A and larger needles, cast on 25 (29, 35) sts.

Row 1 (RS): [K1, inc, k9 (11, 14) sts, inc] twice, k1—29 (33, 39) sts.

Rows 2, 4, 6 and 8: Knit across.

Row 3: [K1, inc, k11 (13, 16) sts, inc] twice, k1—33 (37, 43) sts.

Row 5: [K1, inc, k13 (15, 18) sts, inc] twice, k1—37 (41, 47) sts.

Row 7: K17 (19, 22) sts, inc, k1, inc, k17 (19, 22)—39 (43, 49) sts.

Join C and work 6 rows even in Stripe pat.

Shape instep
Set-up row: With A, k22 (24, 28) sts, k2tog-tbl, turn, leaving rem sts unworked.

Row 1 (WS): Sl 1, p5 (5, 7) sts, p2tog, turn, leaving rem sts unworked.

Row 2 (RS): Sl 1, k5 (5, 7) sts, k2tog-tbl, turn, leaving rem sts unworked.

Rep [Rows 1 and 2] until 9 (11, 10) sts rem on each side—25 (29, 29) sts.

Next row (RS): Turn, knit across instep and next 9 (11, 10) sts.

Next row: Purl across.

Eyelet row: With C, k2, [k2tog, yo] to last st, end k1.

Next row: Purl across.

Cuff
Change to B and smaller needles.

Work in 1/1 Rib for approx 1½ inches, ending with a WS row.

Next row (RS): Purl across for turning ridge.

Continue in 1/1 Rib until cuff measures approx 2½ inches, ending with a WS row.

Bind off.

Finishing
Sew foot and back seam, sewing cuff seam from RS for folded area.

Ties
Using 1 strand each of A, B and C held tog, braid 18- (18-, 19-) inch length for tie. Tie overhand knot at each end and trim ends. Beg and ending at center front, weave tie through eyelet row and tie in bow.

Rep for other bootie. ●

Teddy Bear

The little ones in your life will adore this cute, cuddly bear.

Design by Michelle Wilcox

Skill Level
■■□□ EASY

Finished Size
About 7 inches tall

Materials

- Worsted weight yarn (100% acrylic): 2½ oz/125 yds light brown and small amount light gold
- Small amount black pearl cotton or embroidery floss (for face)
- Size 6 (4mm) needles or size needed to obtain gauge
- Polyester fiberfill

Gauge
14 sts and 24 rows = 4 inches/10cm in St st.

To save time, take time to check gauge.

Special Abbreviation
Knit in front and back (kfb): Inc by knitting in front and back of next st.

Bear

Head
Beg at neck, with light brown, cast on 18 sts.

Row 1: Knit across.

Row 2: Purl across.

Row 3: Kfb of each st across—36 sts.

Row 4: Purl across.

Rows 5–20: [Rep Rows 1 and 2] 8 times.

Row 21: [K2tog] across—18 sts.

Row 22: Purl across.

Row 23: Rep Row 21—9 sts.

Cut yarn, leaving a long end. Draw end through all sts on needle and pull tight to secure. Sew back seam and stuff head. Do not sew neck opening.

Ears
With light brown, cast on 12 sts.

Rows 1–4: Work in St st.

Row 5: [K2tog] across—6 sts.

Row 6: Purl across.

Cut yarn, leaving a long end. Draw yarn through all sts on needle and pull tight to secure. Do not stuff. Sew seam and sew bottom edge flat. Sew in place.

Snout
With light gold, work as for ear. Do not close bottom edge opening but lightly stuff and sew in place on head. Embroider black satin stitch for eyes and nose, and straight stitches for mouth.

Tummy
With light gold, cast on 5 sts.

Row 1: Knit across.

Row 2: Kfb of each st across—10 sts.

Rows 3–14: Knit across.

Row 15: [K2tog] across—5 sts. Bind off.

Body
Beg at bottom of body, with light brown, cast on 12 sts.

Row 1: Knit across.

Row 2: Purl across.

Row 3: Kfb of each st across—24 sts.

Row 4: Purl across.

Row 5: *K3, kfb; rep from * across—30 sts.

Row 6: Purl across.

Cut yarn, leaving a long end. Draw yarn through all sts on needle and pull tight to secure. Sew back seam and stuff body. Attach tummy and sew bottom seam across. Fit neck over top of body and sew in place.

Arms

With light brown, cast on 12 sts.

Row 1: Knit across.

Row 2: Purl across.

Rows 3–8: Rep [Rows 1 and 2] 3 times.

Row 9: [K2tog] across—6 sts.

Row 10: Purl across.

Cut yarn, leaving a long end. Draw yarn through all sts on needle and pull tight to secure. Sew side seam. Stuff and sew in place.

Legs

With light brown, cast on 15 sts.

Row 1: Knit across.

Row 2: Purl across.

Rows 3–10: Rep [Rows 1 and 2] 4 times.

Row 11: [K2tog] 7 times, k1—8 sts.

Row 12: [P2tog] across—4 sts.

Cut yarn, leaving a long end. Draw yarn through all sts on needle and pull tight to secure. Sew side seam. Stuff and sew in place.

Tail

With light brown, cast on 10 sts.

Rows 1–3: Work in St st.

Row 4: [P2tog] across—5 sts.

Cut yarn, leaving a long end. Draw yarn through all sts on needle and pull tight to secure. Sew side seam. Stuff and sew in place at bottom of back body seam. ●

Rows 7–20: Rep [Rows 1 and 2] 7 times.

Row 21: *K3, k2tog; rep from * across—24 sts.

Row 22: Purl across.

Row 23: *K2, k2tog; rep from * across—18 sts.

Row 24: Purl across.

Row 25: *K1, k2tog; rep from * across—12 sts.

Row 26: Purl across.

Teddy Bear Sweater

Dress Teddy up in this simple striped sweater.

Design by Michelle Wilcox

· ·

Skill Level

■■□□ EASY

Finished Size
Fits 7-inch knit animal

Materials
- Sport weight yarn (100% acrylic): ½ oz/25 yds light turquoise (MC) and small amount lime green (CC)
- Size 3 (3.25mm) needles or size needed to obtain gauge

3 LIGHT

Gauge
11 sts = 2 inches/5cm in St st.

To save time, take time to check gauge.

Pattern Note
This sweater is designed to fit Teddy Bear on page 42.

Sweater

Front/Back
Make 2

With MC, cast on 24 sts.

Row 1: *K2, p2; rep from * across.

Rows 2–6: Rep Row 1.

Row 7: Knit across.

Row 8: Purl across.

Rows 9–12: Rep [Rows 7 and 8] twice.

Join CC, do not cut MC.

Rows 13 and 14: With CC, knit across.

Row 15: With MC, knit across.

Row 16: Purl across.

Rows 17 and 18: With CC, knit across. Cut CC.

Row 19: With MC, knit across.

Row 20: Purl across.

Rows 21–28: Rep [Rows 19 and 20] 4 times.

Row 29: Bind off 4 sts, k1, p2, [k2, p2] 3 times, k4—20 sts.

Row 30: Bind off 4 sts, k1, p2, [k2, p2] 3 times— 16 sts.

Rows 31–34: Work in k2, p2 rib for collar. Bind off in ribbing.

Sleeves
With MC, cast on 24 sts.

Row 1: *K2, p2; rep from * across.

Rows 2–6: Rep Row 1.

Bind off in ribbing.

Finishing
Sew neck ribbing and shoulder seams of back and front. Open sweater flat and sew sleeves in place. Sew underarm and side seams. ●

Fun at the Beach: Girl's Set

This 3-piece dress-up ensemble is perfect for an itty-bitty beach babe.

Designs by Frances Hughes

Skill Level
■ ■ □ □ EASY

Finished Sizes
Beach outfit: Fits 5-inch doll
Beach towel: 3½ x 5½ inches

Materials
- Size 5 crochet cotton: 75 yds yellow (A) and 50 yds purple (B)
- Size 3 (3.25mm) knitting needles
- 3 snaps
- Sewing needle and thread
- Small amount of yellow and green embroidery floss
- Felt (for bottom of flip-flops)
- Glue

Gauge
28 sts = 4 inches/10cm in St st.

To save time, take time to check gauge.

Special Abbreviation
Increase (inc): Inc by knitting in front and back of next st.

Pattern Note
Work decreases 1 stitch in from each edge on right-side rows using slip, slip, knit (ssk) decrease at the beginning of the row, and knit 2 together (k2tog) decrease at the end of the row.

Beach Towel
With B, cast on 40 sts.

Border
Knit 4 rows.

Center
Row 1: With A, knit across.

Row 2: K4, purl across to last 4 sts, k4.

Rows 3–6: Rep [Rows 1 and 2] twice.

Rep [Rows 1–6] in following strip sequence:

6 rows B, 6 rows A, 6 rows B, 6 rows A.

Border
With B, knit 4 rows. Bind off.

Bikini Top
Note: Bikini top is worked from side to side.
With B, cast on 3 sts.

Knit 3 rows.

Next row: [Inc] 3 times—6 sts.

Knit 4 rows.

Next row: [K2tog] 3 times—2 sts.

Knit 22 rows.

Next row: [Inc] 3 times—6 sts.

Knit 4 rows.

Next row: [K2tog] 3 times—3 sts.

Knit 3 rows. Bind off.

Sew snap on each end to meet in center front. Referring to photo and using 2 strands of yellow floss held tog, work 7 French knots (see page 125) in a bunch over snap. Using 2 strands of green floss held tog, make 2 lazy daisy sts (see illustration) for leaves.

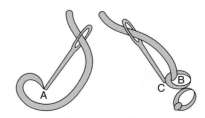

Lazy-Daisy Stitch

Bikini Bottom

Front
With B, cast on 19 sts. Knit 2 rows.

Working in St st, dec 1 st at beg and end of each row until 3 sts rem.

Knit 1 row.

Purl 1 row.

Back
Inc in first and last st every row until there are 17 sts.

Knit 1 row. Bind off.

Sew snap on each side. Embroider flower same as for bikini top on 1 side.

Beach Hat

Brim
With B, cast on 64 sts. Knit 2 rows.

Change to A and beg with knit row, work 6 rows in St st.

Crown
Next row: K2tog across—32 sts.

With B, knit 4 rows.

With A, knit 1 row, and then beg with knit row, work 8 rows in St st.

Next row: K2tog across—16 sts.

Next row: Purl across.

Next row: K2tog across—8 sts.

Next row: Purl across; cut yarn, leaving long end.

Thread end through rem sts and draw up tight to close. Sew side seam of hat and brim.

Flip-Flops
With 2 strands B, cast on 3 sts.

Next row: K1, inc, k1.

Knit 4 rows.

Next row: K1, k2tog, k1.

Knit 4 rows. Bind off.

Cut 4 (10-inch) lengths of A, tie knot in center of these strands. Using 2 strands at a time, tie to bottom of shoe sole approximately ¼-inch apart on each side. Cut 2 pieces of felt and glue to bottom of flip-flop sole to hide knots.

Beach Bag
With B, cast on 15 sts. Knit 4 rows.

Change to A and knit 1 row.

Next row: *P1, yo, p2tog; rep from * across.

Work 14 rows in St st.

Next row: *K1, yo, k2tog; rep from * across.

Purl 1 row.

With B, knit 4 rows. Bind off.

Fold in half and sew sides tog. With B, make 2 (12-inch) lengths of twisted cords. For drawstring, weave cord through yo's each in opposite direction. Knot ends of cord. ●

Snuggle Bug: Boy's Set

Make a little snuggle-bug cocoon and hat for dolly.

Designs by Frances Hughes

. . . .

Skill Level

 EASY

Finished Size
Fits 5-inch doll

Materials
• Size 5 crochet cotton: 75 yds blue
• Size 3 (3.25mm) knitting needles

Gauge
28 sts = 4 inches/10cm in St st.

To save time, take time to check gauge.

Papoose
Note: The 8-st garter border on 1 side forms the collar of the papoose.

Cast on 44 sts.

Row 1: K4, *p4, k4; rep from * to last 8 sts, end k8.

Row 2: K8, p4, *k4, p4; rep from * across.

Rows 3 and 4: Rep Rows 1 and 2.

Row 5: P4, *k4, p4; rep from * to last 8 sts, end k8.

Row 6: K8, k4, *p4, k4; rep from * across.

Rows 7 and 8: Rep Rows 5 and 6.

Rep [Rows 1–8] 6 times.

Bind off.

With RS facing, and beg below 8-st garter edge, sew cast-on and bound-off edges tog. Weave yarn through sts at bottom and pull tightly to close. Fold back garter edge to form collar.

Hat
Cast on 32 sts.

Rows 1 (RS)–4: Knit across.

Rows 5–8: [K4, p4] 4 times.

Rows 9–12: [P4, k4] 4 times.

Row 13: [K2tog] across—16 sts.

Row 14: Purl across.

Row 15: [K2tog] across—8 sts.

Row 16: Purl across.

Cut yarn, leaving a 5-inch end. Weave end through sts and draw up tightly to close. Sew back seam. ●

Loops & Ladders Skullcap

With simple drop-stitch accents, this light and airy skullcap is a simple statement of style.

Design by Kara Gott Warner

Skill Level
■■□□ EASY

Size
1 size fits most

Finished Measurements
Circumference: Approx 21 inches
Height: Approx 7 inches

Materials
- Worsted weight yarn (alpaca/cotton blend): 148 yds walnut
- Size 7 (4.5mm) 16-inch circular and double-point needles (set of 4) or size needed to obtain gauge
- Stitch marker

4 MEDIUM

Gauge
16 sts and 26 rows = 4 inches/10cm in St st.

13 sts and 26 rows = 4 inches/10cm in pat.

To save time, take time to check gauge.

Special Abbreviation
Drop Stitch (DS): Drop st from needle and allow it to unravel to cast-on edge.

Skullcap
Cast on 68 sts, place marker and join without twisting.

Knit 4 rnds.

Work 10 rnds in garter st (purl 1 rnd, knit 1 rnd).

Work in St st (knit every rnd) until cap measures 6 inches.

Next rnd (DS rnd): *K3, DS; rep from * around— 51 sts.

Crown shaping
Note: Change to dpns when sts no longer fit comfortably on circular needle.

Rnd 1: [K2tog] around to last st, k1—26 sts.

Rnd 2: [K2tog] around—13 sts.

Rnd 3: [K2tog] 6 times, k1—7 sts.

Rnd 4: [K2tog] 3 times, k1—4 sts.

Rnd 5: [K2tog] twice—2 sts.

Bind off last 2 sts. Weave end through sts to close opening.

Finishing
Block lightly to finished measurements. ●

Socks for Grandpa

Your thoughtfulness will warm his heart and soul; make some for Grandma too.

Design by Kim Wagner

Skill Level
◼◼◼◻ INTERMEDIATE

Sizes
Adult medium (large) Instructions are given for smaller size, with larger size in parentheses. When only 1 number is given, it applies to both sizes.

Finished Measurement
Cuff length: 6 (7) inches

Materials
- Sock weight yarn (wool/nylon blend): 450 yds/3½ oz brown
- Size 1 (2.5mm) double-point needles (set of 4) or size needed to obtain gauge
- Locking ring stitch marker

1 SUPER FINE

Gauge
32 sts and 46 rnds = 4 inches/10cm in St st in rnds.

To save time, take time to check gauge.

Pattern Stitch
Note: A chart is provided for those preferring to work pat st from a chart.

Seeded Rib (multiple of 6 sts)
Rnd 1: *K2, p3, k1; rep from * around.
Rnd 2: *K1, p1; rep from * around.
Rep Rnds 1 and 2 for pat.

Pattern Note
The amount given in materials list is sufficient for a pair of medium-size socks, with approximately ½ ounce yarn remaining. If knitting for a larger foot, the knitter may choose to shorten the cuff or purchase an additional skein of yarn.

Special Abbreviation
N1, N2, N3: Needle 1, Needle 2, Needle 3.

Sock
Cast on 60 (72) sts and divide sts evenly on 3 dpns—20 (24) sts on each of 3 needles.

Place marker for beg of rnd and join, being careful not to twist sts.

Beg with Rnd 1, work in Seeded Rib pat until sock measures 6 (7) inches or desired length for leg, ending with Rnd 2.

Heel flap

Place first 30 (36) sts onto 1 needle for heel flap, and divide rem 30 (36) sts evenly between 2 needles for instep—15 (18) sts on each of 2 needles.

Work only on 30 (36) heel-flap sts as follows:

Row 1: *Sl 1kwise, k1; rep from * to end of needle, turn.

Row 2: Sl 1pwise, purl across, turn.

Rep Rows 1 and 2 for a total of 29 (35) rows, ending with a RS row.

Heel turn

Row 1 (WS): P17 (20), p2tog, p1, turn.

Row 2: Sl 1kwise, k5, k2tog, k1, turn.

Row 3: Sl 1pwise, purl to last st before turn, p2tog, p1, turn.

Row 4: Sl 1kwise, knit to last st before turn, k2tog, k1, turn.

Rep last 2 rows until all sts have been worked, ending with a knit row—18 (20) sts rem.

Note: Last 2 rows for larger size will end with dec (p2tog/ ssk), with no k1 following.

Gusset

With N1: pick up and knit 15 (18) sts along side of heel flap; N2: work Rnd 1 of pat across 30 (36) instep sts; N3: pick up and knit 15 (18) sts across other side of heel flap plus first 9 (10) sts of heel, slide rem 9 (10) sts onto N1—78 (92) sts.

Center of heel is now beg of rnd. Place marker.

Next rnd: Knit around, keeping instep sts in pat.

Dec rnd: N1: knit to last 3 sts, k2tog, k1; N2: work in pat across; N3: k1, ssk, knit to end.

Rep last 2 rnds until 15 (18) sts rem on N1 and N3—60 (72) sts.

Work even, keeping instep sts in pat until sock measures 2 inches less than desired length.

Shape toe

Rnd 1: N1: knit to last 3 sts, k2tog, k1; N2: k1, ssk, knit to last 3 sts, k2tog, k1; N3: k1, ssk, knit to end.

Rnd 2: Knit all sts.

Rep last 2 rnds until 28 (36) sts rem. With N3, knit across sts on N1—14 (18) sts on each needle. Graft toe sts tog using Kitchener st, page 122. ●

STITCH KEY
□ Knit
− Purl

SEEDED RIB CHART

Stringtown Hat

A little surface texture captures the imagination on the hem of a stylish hat.

Design by Erica Jackofsky

Skill Level
■ ■ ■ ▢ INTERMEDIATE

Sizes
Adult small (medium, large) Instructions are given for smallest size, with larger sizes in parentheses. When only 1 number is given, it applies to all sizes.

Finished Measurement
Circumference: 17½ (20, 22) inches

Materials
- Kraemer Naturally Nazareth (worsted weight; 100% domestic wool; 184 yds/100g per skein): 1 skein moon-light #1322
- Size 5 (3.75mm) 16-inch circular needle or size needed to obtain gauge
- Size 6 (4mm) 16-inch circular needle
- Size 7 (4.5mm) 16-inch circular and double-point needles or size needed to obtain gauge
- 8 stitch markers (1 in different color to mark beg of rnd)

Gauge
22 sts and 36 rnds = 4 inches/10cm in Slipped Rib pat with size 5 needles.

18 sts and 22 rnds = 4 inches/10cm in St st with size 7 needles.

To save time, take time to check gauge.

Special Abbreviation
Slip 2 with yarn in front (sl 2 wyif): Slip 2 sts with yarn held in front of work.

Pattern Stitch
Slipped Rib (multiple of 4 sts)
Rnd 1: *K2, p2; rep from * around.
Rnd 2: *Sl 2 wyif, p2; rep from * around.
Rep Rnds 1 and 2 for pat.

Hat
With size 5 needle, cast on 96 (112, 120) sts. Place marker for beg of rnd and join, taking care not to twist sts.

Work in Slipped Rib pat until hat measures 2 inches from beg.

Change to size 6 needles and continue in established pat until hat measures 3 inches.

Next rnd: Knit around.

Next rnd: *Sl 2 wyif, p2; rep from * around.

Rep last 2 rnds until hat measures 4 inches from beg.

Change to size 7 needles.

Rnd 1: Knit around.

Rnd 2: *Sl 2 wyif, k6; rep from * around.

Rnds 3 and 4: Rep Rnds 1 and 2.

Rnds 5 and 6: Knit around.

Rnd 7: *Sl 2 wyif, k6; rep from * around.

Rnds 8–10: Knit around.

Rnd 11: *Sl 2 wyif, k6; rep from * around.

Beg on next rnd, work even in St st (knit every rnd) until hat measures 7 (7½, 7½) inches from beg.

Shape crown
Note: Change to dpns as needed.

Set-up rnd: [K12 (14, 15), place marker] 7 times, k12 (14, 15).

Dec rnd: [Knit to 2 sts before marker, k2tog, slip marker] 8 times—8 sts dec.

Rep Dec rnd until 16 sts rem.

Next rnd: [K2tog] 8 times, removing all markers— 8 sts rem.

Cut yarn and weave end through rem sts, fasten off securely. Block if desired. ●

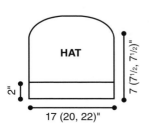

Infinity & Beyond Scarf

This chunky cowl knits up in a flash. Just twist, fold or roll the scarf into your desired look, pop one or both of the buttons through a dropped stitch, and you're ready to hit the catwalk!

Design by Sarah Wilson

. . . .

Skill Level

■□□□ BEGINNER

Finished Size
Circumference: 26 inches
Width: 8 inches

Materials
- Plymouth Baby Alpaca Grande (chunky weight; 100% baby alpaca; 110 yards/100g per skein): 1 skein brown #302
- Size 11 (8mm) 16-inch circular needle or size needed to obtain gauge
- Stitch marker
- 2 (2½-inch) buttons
- Sewing needle and matching thread

5 BULKY

Gauge
11 sts and 21 rows = 4 inches/10cm in garter st.

To save time, take time to check gauge.

Pattern Note
Scarf can be made using 2 circular needles or Magic Loop method if preferred.

Scarf
Cast on 48 sts. Place marker for beg of rnd and join, being careful not to twist sts.

Work in garter st (knit 1 rnd, purl 1 rnd) until piece measures 8 inches from cast-on edge.

Bind off as follows: *Bind off 4 sts, draw up a large loop from last bound-off st and pass entire ball of yarn through loop, drawing close to secure st; drop next st off needle and allow it to unravel down to cast-on row; loosely carry yarn across dropped st; rep from * around.

Finishing

Stretch gently to ensure all dropped sts have unraveled.

Sew on buttons. Twist, fold or roll scarf as desired, using drop-st area for buttonholes. ●

Butterfly Garden Socks

Tickle your fancy with flowers and butterflies on your socks to warm your toes.

Design by Paige Sylvester

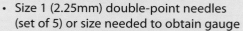

Skill Level
■■■□ INTERMEDIATE

Finished Size
Woman's, 1 size fits most

Materials
- Madelinetosh Tosh Sock (sock weight; 100% superwash merino wool; 395 yds per skein): 1 skein seaglass
- Size 1 (2.25mm) double-point needles (set of 5) or size needed to obtain gauge
- Size 11 (1.10mm) steel crochet hook
- Stitch markers
- 20g E beads in green, yellow and petal color(s) of choice

1 SUPER FINE

Gauge
32 sts = 4 inches/10cm in St st.

To save time, take time to check gauge.

Special Abbreviations
N1, N2, N3, N4: Needle 1, Needle 2, Needle 3, Needle 4.

Pattern Stitch
Butterfly Motif (worked over 5 sts)
Rows 1, 3, 5, 7 and 9: Slip next 5 sts individually wyif.
Rows 2, 4, 6 and 8: K5.
Row 10: K2, insert RH needle under 5 strands of yarn and work next st over 5 strands, k2.

Special Technique
Beads: To add a bead, place crochet hook through bead, take st to be beaded (before you knit it) and put st on crochet hook, slowly pull bead down over st. Knit st as normal.

Pattern Note
Slip all stitches purlwise.

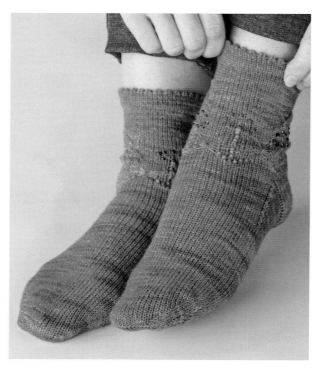

Sock

Leg
Loosely cast on 64 sts, leaving a 24-inch tail. Place 16 sts on each of 4 needles. Place marker for beg of rnd and join without twisting.

Rnds 1–8: Knit around.

Rnd 9 (turning rnd): *Yo, k2tog; rep from * around.

Rnds 10–30: Knit around.

Rnds 31–60: Work Rnds 1–30 of chart.

Note: While working chart, it may be necessary to move sts from needle to needle in order to work Butterfly Motifs. Before working heel flap, be sure to return sts to original number of 16 sts on each needle.

Rnds 61–64: Knit around.

Heel flap

Knit sts from N1 onto N4—32 sts on N4 for heel flap, 16 sts each on N2 and N3 for instep.

Working on heel flap sts only:

Row 1 (WS): Sl 1, purl across.

Row 2 (RS): *Sl 1, k1; rep from * across.

Row 3: Sl 1, purl across.

Rep [Rows 2 and 3] 15 times more.

Turning heel

Row 1 (RS): Sl 1, k20, ssk, turn, leaving rem sts unworked.

Row 2: Sl 1, p10, p2tog, turn, leaving rem sts unworked—30 sts.

Row 3: Sl 1, k10, ssk, turn.

Row 4: Sl 1, p10, p2tog, turn.

Rep Rows 3 and 4 until 12 sts rem.

Next row: K12, on same needle, pick up and knit 18 sts along side of heel flap; knit across N2 and N3; with free needle, pick up and knit 18 sts along other side of heel flap—80 sts.

Arrange sts as follows: N1: 24 sts; N2 and N3: 16 sts each needle; N4: 24 sts; join to work in rnds.

Gusset

Rnd 1: Knit around, knitting picked-up sts tbl.

Rnd 2: N1: knit to last 3 sts, k2tog, k1; N2 and N3: knit across; N4: k1, ssk, knit to end of row.

Rnd 3: Knit around.

Rep Rnds 2 and 3 until 16 sts rem on each of 4 needles—64 sts.

Foot

Knit even in St st until foot measures 1½ inches less than desired length (generally between the first and 2nd knuckle on your big toe).

Toe

Rnd 1: N1: knit to last 3 sts, k2tog, k1; N2: k1, ssk, knit to end of needle; N3: knit to last 3 sts, k2tog, k1; N4: k1, ssk, knit to end of needle.

Rnd 2: Knit around.

Rep Rnds 1 and 2 until 7 sts rem on each needle.

Knit sts on N1 onto N4; slide sts from N2 onto N3.

Holding sts parallel, graft toe tog using Kitchener st, page 122.

Finishing

Turn top edge on picot turning rnd and tack in place. Block. ●

STITCH KEY

- ☐ K on RS, p on WS
- ⱴ Slip st pwise wyif
- ▨ Bead color of choice for petal
- ▨ Green bead for stem and leaf
- ☐ Yellow bead
- On 10th row of motif insert RH needle under 5 strands on RS, and knit tog with next st on LH needle

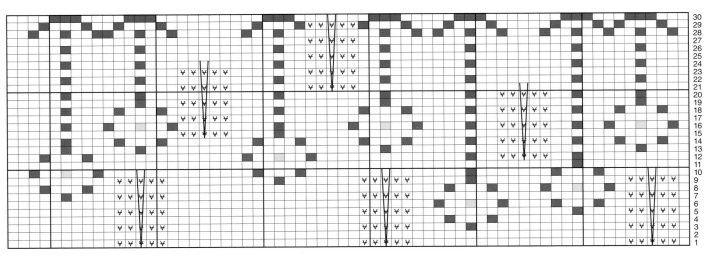

BUTTERFLY GARDEN CHART

Lovely Lace Clutch

A fanciful flap grows into a small clutch bag.

Design by Lois Young

Skill Level
■■■■ EXPERIENCED

Size
7¾ x 4¾ inches (folded)

Finished Measurements
Circumference: 12 inches
Height: Approx 9½ inches

Materials
- Alchemy Yarns Monarch (fingering weight; 70% cashmere/30% silk; 156 yds/40g per ball): 1 ball cherry tart #44F
- Size 3 (3.25mm) needles or size needed to obtain gauge
- Stitch markers
- Contrasting-color lining fabric: 9 x 20-inch piece
- 3 snap fasteners

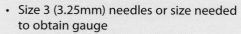

SUPER FINE

Gauge
21 sts and 32 rows = 4 inches/10cm in pat (after blocking).

To save time, take time to check gauge.

Pattern Stitches
Clutch Lace (multiple of 8 sts + 1)
Row 1 (RS): K4, *yo, ssk, k6; rep from * to last 5 sts, end yo, ssk, k3.
Row 2: P3, *yo, p2tog, p6; rep from * to last 5 sts, end yo, p2tog, p4.
Rep Rows 1 and 2 for pat.

Lovely Lace
Work according to chart.

Pattern Note

On wrong-side row, work purl 1, knit 1 in double yarn over.

Flap

Cast on 14 sts. Knit 1 row.

Work [Rows 1–12 of chart] 5 times.

Knit 1 row. Bind off kwise.

Purse

With RS facing, pick up and knit 41 sts across straight edge of lace.

Knit 1 row. Mark each end of this row.

Beg Clutch Lace pat and work until clutch measures 9¼ inches from marked row, ending with a RS row. Knit 2 rows, bind off kwise on WS.

Assembly

Wet lace, stretch and pin out to required dimension.

Lining

Cut 2 pieces of lining fabric the width and length of knitted piece plus ¼-inch seam allowance on all sides. With RS of lining tog, trace flap pat at 1 end. Sew flap, following pattern line, and side seams, leaving other short end open. Trim points, turn lining to RS and press. Place on knitted piece, with lining just below edge of points; mark flap and straight end for length. Turn seam allowance to inside and sew seam. Fold bottom of lining to flap line, sew side seams.

Fold straight edge of purse up to flap line, sew side seams. Insert lining into purse, sew in place across front and around edge of flap; sew 3 snaps to top of flap and front of purse. ●

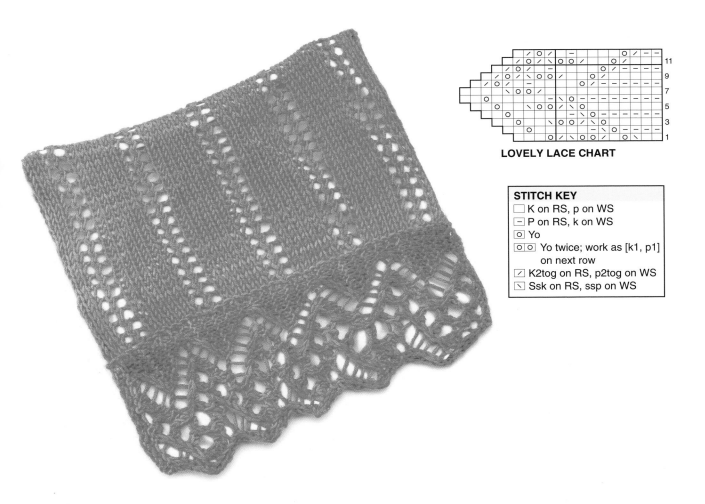

LOVELY LACE CHART

STITCH KEY
- ☐ K on RS, p on WS
- ⊟ P on RS, k on WS
- ☉ Yo
- ☉☉ Yo twice; work as [k1, p1] on next row
- ⟋ K2tog on RS, p2tog on WS
- ⟍ Ssk on RS, ssp on WS

Plissados Scarf

It's all about the ruffles—fun, flirty and flattering.

Design by Jean Clement

Skill Level
■■□□ EASY

Finished Size
Approx 12 x 31 inches

Materials

- Malabrigo Sock (fingering weight; 100% superwash merino wool; 440 yds/100g per skein): 1 skein lettuce #37
- Size 7 (4.5mm) 40-inch circular needle or size needed to obtain gauge
- Optional Coconut Brown shawl pin available on AnniesAttic.com

Gauge
23 sts and 24 rows = 4 inches/10cm in St st.

To save time, take time to check gauge.

Pattern Notes
This scarf uses the entire skein of yarn; therefore, achieving the correct gauge is important.

Circular needle is used to accommodate large number of stitches. Do not join; work back and forth in rows.

All stitches are slipped purlwise.

To obtain the ruffling shape of this scarf, multiple increases are made on every right-side row. As number of stitches quickly becomes rather large, the stitch count is not given on every right-side row.

Scarf
Cast on 19 sts and leave a 12-inch tail. Knit 1 row using both working yarn and cast-on tail.

Row 1 (RS): Sl 1, k2, [yo, k1, yo, k3] 4 times (8 sts inc).

Row 2 and all WS rows: Purl across.

Row 3: Sl 1, k2, *yo, k3, yo, k3; rep from * across.

Row 5: Sl 1, k2, *yo, k5, yo, k3; rep from * across.

Row 7: Sl 1, k2, *yo, k7, yo, k3; rep from * across.

Row 9: Sl 1, k2, *yo, k9, yo, k3; rep from * across.

Row 11: Sl 1, k2, *yo, k11, yo, k3; rep from * across.

Row 13: Sl 1, k2, *yo, k13, yo, k3; rep from * across.

Row 15: Sl 1, k2, *yo, k15, yo, k3; rep from * across.

Row 17: Sl 1, k2, *yo, k17, yo, k3; rep from * across—91 sts.

Row 19: Sl 1, k2, *yo, k9, yo, k1, yo, k9, yo, k3; rep from * across (16 sts inc).

Row 21: Sl 1, k2, *yo, k10, yo, k3, yo, k10, yo, k3; rep from * across.

Row 23: Sl 1, k2, *yo, k11, yo, k5, yo, k11, yo, k3; rep from * across.

Row 25: Sl 1, k2, *yo, k12, yo, k7, yo, k12, yo, k3; rep from * across.

Row 27: Sl 1, k2, *yo, k13, yo, k9, yo, k13, yo, k3; rep from * across.

Row 29: Sl 1, k2, *yo, k14, yo, k11, yo, k14, yo, k3; rep from * across.

Row 31: Sl 1, k2, *yo, k15, yo, k13, yo, k15, yo, k3; rep from * across.

Row 33: Sl 1, k2, *yo, k16, yo, k15, yo, k16, yo, k3; rep from * across.

Row 35: Sl 1, k2, *yo, k17, yo, k17, yo, k17, yo, k3; rep from * across—235 sts.

Row 37: Sl 1, k2, *yo, k18, yo, k9, yo, k1, yo, k9, yo, k18, yo, k3; rep from * across (24 sts inc).

Row 39: Sl 1, k2, *yo, k19, yo, k10, yo, k3, yo, k10, yo, k19, yo, k3; rep from * across.

Row 41: Sl 1, k2, *yo, k20, yo, k11, yo, k5, yo, k11, yo, k20, yo, k3; rep from * across.

Row 43: Sl 1, k2, *yo, k21, yo, k12, yo, k7, yo, k12, yo, k21, yo, k3; rep from * across.

Row 45: Sl 1, k2, *yo, k22, yo, k13, yo, k9, yo, k13, yo, k22, yo, k3; rep from * across.

Row 47: Sl 1, k2, *yo, k23, yo, k14, yo, k11, yo, k14, yo, k22, yo, k3; rep from * across.

Row 49: Sl 1, k2, *yo, k24, yo, k15, yo, k13, yo, k15, yo, k24, yo, k3; rep from * across.

Row 51: Sl 1, k2, *yo, k25, yo, k16, yo, k15, yo, k16, yo, k26, yo, k3; rep from * across.

Row 53: Sl 1, k2, *yo, k26, yo, k17, yo, k17, yo, k17, yo, k26, yo, k3; rep from * across—451 sts.

Row 55: Sl 1, k2, *yo, k27, yo, k18, yo, k9, yo, k1, yo, k9, yo, k18, yo, k27, yo, k3; rep from * across (32 sts inc).

Row 57: Sl 1, k2, *yo, k28, yo, k19, yo, k10, yo, k3, yo, k10, yo, k19, yo, k28, yo, k3; rep from * across.

Row 59: Sl 1, k2, *yo, k29, yo, k20, yo, k11, yo, k5, yo, k11, yo, k20, yo, k29, yo, k3; rep from * across.

Row 61: Sl 1, k2, *yo, k30, yo, k21, yo, k12, yo, k7, yo, k12, yo, k21, yo, k30, yo, k3; rep from * across.

Row 63: Sl 1, k2, *yo, k31, yo, k22, yo, k13, yo, k9, yo, k13, yo, k22, yo, k31, yo, k3; rep from * across.

Row 65: Sl 1, k2, *yo, k32, yo, k23, yo, k14, yo, k11, yo, k14, yo, k23, yo, k32, yo, k3; rep from * across—643 sts.

Row 66: Purl across.

Border

Row 1 (RS): Sl 1, k2, *[yo, k3] 26 times, yo, k1, [yo, k3] 27 times; rep from * across—859 sts.

Row 2: Purl across.

Row 3: Sl 1, *k1, yo; rep from * to last 2 sts, k2—1,715 sts.

Bind off as follows: *P2tog, 1 st on RH needle, slip st back to LH needle; rep from * across. Fasten off.

Finishing
Block gently. ●

Meanderlust

This neck warmer makes full use of the unique qualities of thick and thin yarn with a straightforward cable pattern and lace edging.

Design by Linda Wilgus

Skill Level

■ ■ ■ ☐ INTERMEDIATE

Finished Size
Approx 6½ x 22 inches

Materials
• Cascade Yarn Jewel (chunky weight; 100% Peruvian wool; 142 yds/ 100g per skein): 1 skein tan #9263
• Size 9 (5.5mm) needles or size needed to obtain gauge
• 2 (1½-inch) buttons
• Cable needle

Gauge
23 sts and 21 rows = 4 inches/10cm in Honeycomb Cable pat.

To save time, take time to check gauge.

Special Abbreviations
Cable over 4 front (C4F): Slip next 2 sts on cn and hold to front, k2, k2 from cn.

Cable over 4 back (C4B): Slip next 2 sts on cn and hold to back, k2, k2 from cn.

Pattern Stitches
Note: Charts are provided for those preferring to work pattern sts from a chart.

Honeycomb Cable (worked over 24 sts)
Row 1 (RS): K2, p2, [C4B, C4F] twice, p2, k2.
Rows 2, 4 and 6: P2, k2, purl to last 4 sts, k2, p2.
Rows 3 and 7: K2, p2, knit to last 4 sts, p2, k2.
Row 5: K2, p2, [C4F, C4B] twice, p2, k2.
Row 8: P2, k2, purl to last 4 sts, k2, p2.
Rep Rows 1–8 for pat.

Lace Edging
Row 1 (RS): K2, yo, k2tog, yo, k2—7 sts.
Row 2: K2, [yo, k1] twice, yo, k2tog, k1—9 sts.
Row 3: K2, yo, k2tog, yo, k3, yo, k2—11 sts.
Row 4: K2, yo, k5, yo, k1, yo, k2tog, k1—13 sts.
Row 5: K2, yo, k2tog, yo, ssk, k3, k2tog, yo, k2.
Row 6: K3, yo, ssk, k1, k2tog, yo, k2, yo, k2tog, k1.
Row 7: K2, yo, k2tog, k2, yo, sk2p, yo, k4.
Row 8: Bind off 7 sts, k3 (including st on needle after bind-off), yo, k2tog, k1—6 sts.
Rep Rows 1–8 for pat.

Special Technique
Cable Cast-On: Place needle with last st worked in LH. Knit st but do not drop st from needle. Insert LH needle in the front loop of new st and transfer to LH needle. *Insert RH needle between new st and old st and knit a st. Transfer new st to LH needle as before. Rep from * for desired number of sts.

Scarf
Cast on 24 sts.

Set-up row (WS): P2, k2, purl to last 4 sts, k2, p2.

Work [Rows 1–8 of Honeycomb Cable pat] 14 times.

Note: Scarf should measure approx 19 inches.

Buttonholes
Row 1 (RS): K2, p2, [C4B, C4F] twice, p2, k2.

Row 2: P2, k2, p2, bind off the next 4 sts, p4 (including st on needle after bind-off), bind off the next 4 sts, p2 (including st on needle after bind-off), k2, p2—16 sts.

Row 3: K2, p2, k2, cast on 4 sts using Cable Cast-On, k4, cast on 4 sts using Cable Cast-On, k2, p2, k2—20 sts.

Rows 4 and 6: P2, k2, purl to last 4 sts, k2, p2.

Row 5: K2, p2, [C4F, C4B] twice, p2, k2.

Row 7: K2, p2, knit to last 4 sts, p2, k2.

Row 8: P2, k2, purl to last 4 sts, k2, p2.

Work Rows 1–8 of Honeycomb Cable pat until scarf measures 22 inches.

Bind off all sts.

Edging
Cast on 6 sts.

Knit 1 row.

Work Rows 1–8 of Lace Edging pat until edging measures 22 inches, ending with a Row 8.
Bind off all sts.

Finishing
Place scarf flat with RS facing and buttonholes to right. Place lace edging flat along bottom long edge and sew in place. Attach buttons, as desired, opposite buttonholes. ●

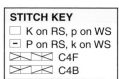

STITCH KEY
☐ K on RS, p on WS
⊟ P on RS, k on WS
Ⓞ Yo
⬈ K2tog
⬊ Ssk
⬈ Sk2p
⋂ Bind off
■ No st

LACE EDGING CHART

STITCH KEY
☐ K on RS, p on WS
⊟ P on RS, k on WS
⬛⬛ C4F
⬛⬛ C4B

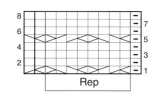
Rep

HONEYCOMB CABLE CHART

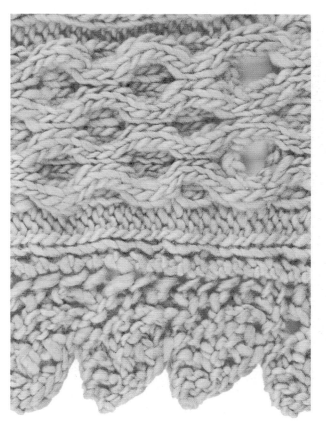

Windowpanes of Color Beanie

This unique cap incorporates three colors, just one skein each to make this easy-to-wear design.

Design by Edie Eckman

....

Skill Level

■■■□ INTERMEDIATE

Size
Fits 22–23-inch-circumference head

Finished Measurements
Circumference: 19 inches (unstretched)
Height: Approx 9½ inches

Materials
- Patons Classic Wool (worsted weight; 100% wool; 210 yds/100g per ball): 1 ball each dark gray mix #00225 (A), paprika #00238 (B), wisteria #77308 (C) and leaf green #00240 (D)
- Size 7 (4.5mm) 16-inch circular and double-point needles or size needed to obtain gauge
- Stitch marker

Gauge
20 sts and 32 rows = 4 inch/10cm in Windowpane Stripe pat.

To save time, take time to check gauge.

Pattern Stitch
Windowpane Stripe
Rnd 1: With A, knit around.
Rnd 2: Purl around.
Rnds 3 and 4: With B, [k3, sl 1] around.
Rnds 5 and 6: With A, rep Rnds 1 and 2.
Rnds 7 and 8: With D, rep Rnds 3 and 4.
Rnds 9 and 10: With A, rep Rnds 1 and 2.
Rnds 11 and 12: With C, rep Rnds 3 and 4.
Rep Rnds 1–12 for pat.

Pattern Note
Slip all stitches purlwise unless otherwise stated.

Beanie

Body
With circular needle and A, cast on 96 sts. Place marker for beg of rnd and join, being careful not to twist sts.

Rnd 1: Purl around.

Rnd 2: With B, [k3, sl 1] around.

Rnd 3: [P3, sl 1 wyib] around.

Rnd 4: With A, knit around.

Rnd 5: Purl around.

Rnd 6: With C, [k1, sl 1, k2] around.

Rnd 7: [P1, sl 1 wyib, p2] around.

Rnd 8: With A, knit around.

Rnd 9: Purl around.

Rnds 10 and 11: With D, rep Rnd 2.

Rnds 12 and 13: With B, rep Rnds 6 and 7.

Rnds 14 and 15: With C, rep Rnd 2.

Work [Rnds 1–12 of Windowpane Stripe pat] twice.

Work Rnds 1–6 of Windowpane Stripe pat.

Shape top
Note: *Change to dpns, as necessary, when sts no longer fit comfortably on circular needle.*

Rnd 1: With D, knit around.

Rnd 2: [K4, ssk] around—80 sts.

Rnd 3: With A, knit around.

Rnd 4: Purl around.

Rnd 5: With C, knit around.

Rnd 6: [K3, k2tog] around—64 sts.

Rnds 7 and 8: Rep Rnds 3 and 4.

Rnd 9: With B, knit around.

Rnd 10: [K2, ssk] around—48 sts.

Rnd 11: With A, knit around.

Rnd 12: [P1, p2tog] around—32 sts.

Rnd 13: With D, knit around.

Rnd 14: [K2tog] around—16 sts.

Rnd 15: With A, knit around.

Rnd 16: [P2tog] around—8 sts.

Cut yarn, leaving a long end. Weave end through rem sts. Pull tight to close circle. ●

Springtime Beret

Keep your shining mane tamed with a soft little beret of lace!

Design by Cecily Glowik MacDonald

Skill Level
■■■□ INTERMEDIATE

Size
Woman's, 1 size fits most

Finished Measurement
Circumference: Approx 20 inches (slightly stretched)

Materials
- Classic Elite Verde Collection Sprout (bulky weight; 100% organic cotton; 109 yds/100g per hank): 1 hank natural #4316
- Size 8 (5mm) 16-inch circular needle
- Size 10 (6mm) 16-inch circular and set of double-point needles or size needed to obtain gauge
- Stitch markers

Gauge
14 sts and 22 rows = 4 inches/10cm in St st with larger needles.

To save time, take time to check gauge.

Pattern Stitches
1/1 Rib (even number of sts)
Rnd 1: *K1, p1; rep from * around.
Rep Rnd 1 for pat.

Rev St st (any number of sts)
Purl all rnds.

Lace Panel (panel of 14 sts)
Rnd 1: Yo, k3, ssk, k9.
Rnd 2: K1, yo, k3, ssk, k8.
Rnd 3: K2, yo, k3, ssk, k7.
Rnd 4: K3, yo, k3, ssk, k6.
Rnd 5: K4, yo, k3, ssk, k5.
Rnd 6: K5, yo, k3, ssk, k4.
Rnd 7: K6, yo, k3, ssk, k3.
Rnd 8: K7, yo, k3, ssk, k2.
Rnd 9: K8, yo, k3, ssk, k1.

Rnd 10: K9, yo, k3, ssk.
Rep Rnds 1–10 for Lace Panel.

Beret
With smaller needles, cast on 72 sts. Mark beg of rnd and join without twisting.

Work 5 rnds even in 1/1 Rib pat.

Change to larger needles.

Set-up rnd: [Work 10 sts in Rev St st pat, place marker, work Rnd 1 of Lace Panel pat over next 14 sts, place marker] 3 times.

Note: Slip markers as you come to them.

Work even in established pat until beret measures 5 inches from beg.

Shape top
Notes: Continue established Lace Panel pat in Rnds 1–4 below. Change to dpns when sts no longer fit comfortably on circular needle.

Rnd 1: [P2tog, p6, p2tog, work Lace Panel] 3 times—66 sts.

Rnd 2: [P2tog, p4, p2tog, work Lace Panel] 3 times—60 sts.

Rnd 3: [P2tog, p2, p2tog, work Lace Panel] 3 times—54 sts.

Rnd 4: [P2tog twice, work Lace Panel] 3 times—48 sts.

Rnd 5: [P2, ssk, k10, k2tog] 3 times—42 sts.

Rnd 6: [P2, ssk, k8, k2tog] 3 times—36 sts.

Rnd 7: [P2, ssk, k6, k2tog] 3 times—30 sts.

Rnd 8: [P2, ssk, k4, k2tog] 3 times—24 sts.

Rnd 9: [P2, ssk, k2, k2tog] 3 times—18 sts.

Rnd 10: [P2, ssk, k2tog] 3 times—12 sts.

Rnd 11: [P2tog, remove marker, ssk, remove marker] 3 times—6 sts.

Cut yarn, leaving a 6-inch end. Weave end through rem sts and pull tightly to close top of beret.

Block beret over 10-inch dinner plate. ●

Added Spice Scarf

Just four colors, one ball each, of textured yarn from your stash will make this intriguing scarf.

Design by Cynthia Adams

Skill Level
 EASY

Finished Size
Approx 5 x 68 inches

Materials
- Worsted weight yarn: 275 yds each persimmon (A) and red (C)
- Bulky weight novelty yarn: 90 yds tan (B)
- Worsted weight brushed yarn: 300 yds persimmon (D)
- Size 10 (6mm) needles or size needed to obtain gauge

4 MEDIUM

5 BULKY

Gauge
12 sts = 4 inches/10cm in garter st.

Gauge is not critical to this project.

Special Abbreviation
Increase (inc): Inc by knitting in front and back of st.

Pattern Notes
Change colors on right-side rows. Work increases and decreases on wrong-side rows.

Slip all stitches purlwise.

Scarf
With A, cast on 20 sts.

Row 1 (RS): Sl 1 wyif, knit across.

Row 2: Sl 1 wyif, inc, k15, k2tog, k1.

Rows 3–10: Rep [Rows 1 and 2] 4 times. Fasten off.

Rows 11–20: With B, rep Rows 1–10.

Rows 21–30: With C, rep Rows 1–10.

Rows 31–40: With D, rep rows 1–10. Rep [Rows 1–40] 5 times.

With A, rep Rows 1–10.

Bind off and weave in ends. ●

It Takes Two

This chapter broadens your horizons for ways to knit great items with just two skeins. Add a little drama to that little black dress with our easy shrug or moebius. You'll keep baby warm and snuggly in our color-block baby afghan in three different colors, each calling for just two balls per color.

Mad-for-Plaid Blanket

Turn stripes into plaid by adding simple slip-stitch verticals.

Design by Colleen Smitherman

Skill Level
■■□□ EASY

Finished Size
Approx 30 x 30 inches

Materials
- Plymouth Encore Worsted (worsted weight; 75% acrylic/25% wool; 200 yds/100g per ball): 2 balls each light green #3335 (A), natural #256 (B) and blue #4045 (C)
- Size 7 (4.5mm) 36-inch circular needle or size needed to obtain gauge
- Stitch markers
- Size G/6 (4mm) crochet hook
- Size L/11 (8mm) crochet hook
- Row counter (optional)

4 MEDIUM

Gauge
16 sts and 27 rows = 4 inches/10cm in St st.

To save time, take time to check gauge.

Pattern Notes
Circular needle is used to accommodate large number of stitches. Do not join; work back and forth in rows.

Slip all stitches purlwise.

Blanket

Band 1
With A, cast on 97 sts.

Row 1 (RS): K2, *p1, k1; rep from * to last st, end sl 1.

Row 2: P2, *k1, p1; rep from * to last st, end sl 1.

Rows 3–8: Rep [Rows 1 and 2] 3 times.

Row 9: K2, [p1, k1] 3 times, place marker, [p16, k16] twice, p17, place marker, [k1, p1] 3 times, end k1, sl 1.

Note: Slip markers as you come to them on following rows.

Row 10: P2, [k1, p1] 3 times, k17, [p16, k16] twice, [p1, k1] 3 times, end p1, sl 1.

Rows 11–34: Rep [Rows 9 and 10] 12 times.

Band 2
Change to B.

Row 1 (RS): K2, [p1, k1] 3 times, [k16, p16] twice, k17, [k1, p1] 3 times, end k1, sl 1.

Row 2: P2, [k1, p1] 3 times, p17, [k16, p16] twice, [p1, k1] 3 times, end p1, sl 1.

Rows 3–34: Rep [Rows 1 and 2] 16 times.

Band 3
Change to C.

Row 1 (RS): K2, [p1, k1] 3 times, [k16, k16] twice, p17, [k1, p1] 3 times, end k1, sl 1.

Row 2: P2, [k1, p1] 3 times, k17, [p16, k16] twice, [p1, k1] 3 times, end p1, sl 1.

Rows 3–34: Rep [Rows 1 and 2] 16 times.

Band 4
Change to A, rep Band 2.

Band 5
Change to B, rep Band 3.

Band 6
Change to C, work Rows 1–26 of Band 2.

Row 27 (RS): K2, *p1, k1; rep from * to last st, end sl 1.

Row 28: P2, *k1, p1; rep from * to last st, end sl 1.

Rows 29–34: Rep [Rows 27 and 28] 3 times.

Drop-Stitch Bind-Off

Note: *If not familiar with crocheted chain st (ch), see illustration on page 122.*

Bind off 7 sts. *Move last st on RH needle onto smaller crochet hook, ch 4, place crochet loop on RH needle, drop next st from LH needle, bind off next 7 sts; rep from * until 8 sts rem on LH needle. Move st on RH needle onto hook, ch 4, place last crochet loop on RH needle, drop next st from LH needle, bind off rem 7 sts.

Vertical Decorative Chains

Unravel all dropped sts from top to bottom of blanket, forming 11 vertical ladders. Beg with ladder at lower left, with A, place slip knot on larger crochet hook. Holding yarn behind blanket and crochet hook on top of blanket, insert hook between 2nd and 3rd steps in ladder and pull up a loop of yarn from back to front of blanket. Pull loop through loop on hook (first ch made). Continue making chs up ladder 2 steps at a time, keeping decorative chain on RS of ladder and taking care to keep blanket flat.

*When last ch is made in last steps, turn blanket over and move hook to top and yarn to bottom of blanket. Work another column of chs as before on opposite side next to last decorative chain, moving up ladder 2 steps at a time. Rep from * once more.

Work decorative chains in same manner across blanket in rem dropped-st ladders in following sequence: [B, C, B, A] twice, end B, C. ●

Pumpkin Seeds Vest

Cute cables mimic pumpkins on a background of seed stitches.

Design by Trish Warrick

Skill Level
■□□□ **EASY**

Sizes
Child's size 2 (4, 6, 8, 10) Instructions are given for smallest size, with larger sizes in parentheses. When only 1 number is given, it applies to all sizes.

Finished Measurements
Chest: 24 (27, 31, 34¼, 37¾) inches
Length: 12¾ (13¾, 15¼, 17¾, 20¾) inches

Materials
- Plymouth Encore Worsted (worsted weight; 75% acrylic/25% wool; 200 yds/100g per ball): 2 (2, 3, 3, 3) balls rust #456
- Size 8 (5mm) circular needle or size needed to obtain gauge
- Cable needle
- Stitch holders
- 3 (3, 4, 4, 4) ⅞-inch buttons

Gauge
19 sts and 26 rows = 4 inches/10cm in Seed St pat.

To save time, take time to check gauge.

Special Abbreviations
Cable 8 Front (C8F): Slip next 4 sts to cn and hold in front, p3, k1, then k4 from cn.

Cable 8 Back (C8B): Slip next 4 sts to cn and hold in back, k4, then k1, p3 from cn.

Slip, slip, purl (ssp): Slip next 2 sts, 1 at a time, kwise from LH to RH needle; slip sts back to LH needle keeping them twisted, p2tog-tbl.

Pattern Stitch
Seed Stitch (odd number of sts)
Row 1: [P1, k1] across to last st, p1.

Row 2: Knit the purl sts and purl the knit sts.
Rep Row 2 for pat.

Pattern Notes
Vest is worked back and forth in 1 piece to armholes. A circular needle is used to accommodate the large number of stitches.

Seed stitch spreads, but ribs and cables draw in, so decreases are made when changing patterns. The armhole and neck shaping is worked in the Seed Stitch pattern sections.

To maintain pattern, when 2nd stitch on left-hand needle is a knit stitch, use a purl decrease, and when 2nd stitch on left hand needle is a purl stitch, use a knit decrease.

Body
Beg at lower edge, cast on 136 (155, 174, 193, 212) sts, using cable cast-on (see page 120).

Row 1 (RS): P3, [k4, p3, k2, p3, k4, p3] 7 (8, 9, 10, 11) times.

Row 2: K3, [p4, k3, p2, k3, p4, k3] 7 (8, 9, 10, 11) times.

Rows 3–10: Rep [Rows 1 and 2] 4 times.

Row 11: P3, *C8F, C8B, p3; rep from * across.

Row 12: K6, p10, *k9, p10; rep from * to last 6 sts, end k6.

Row 13: P9, k4, *p15, k4; rep from * to last 9 sts, end p9.

Row 14: K9, p1, p2tog, p1, *k15, p1, p2tog, p1; rep from * to last 9 sts, end k9—129 (147, 165, 183, 201) sts.

Row 15: Work 7 sts in Seed St pat, p2, k1, p1, k1, p2, *work 11 sts in Seed St pat, p2, k1, p1, k1, p2; rep from * to last 7 sts, work last 7 sts in Seed St pat.

Row 16: Work 7 sts in Seed St pat, k2, p1, k1, p1, k2, *work 11 sts in Seed St pat, k2, p1, k1, p1, k2; rep from * to last 7 sts, work last 7 sts in Seed St pat.

Rep Rows 15 and 16 until body measures 7 (7½, 8½, 10, 12) inches or desired length to armhole, ending with a WS row.

Next row (RS): Work 7 sts in Seed St pat, p2tog, k1, p1, k1, p2tog, *work 11 sts in Seed St pat, p2tog, k1, p1, k1, p2tog; rep from * to last 7 sts, work last 7 sts in Seed St pat—115 (131, 147, 163, 179) sts.

Next row: Work 29 (33, 37, 41, 45) sts in Seed St pat for left front, place marker for armhole; work next 57 (65, 73, 81, 89) sts in Seed St pat for back, place marker for armhole; work last 29 (33, 37, 41, 45) sts in Seed St pat for right front.

Divide fronts & back
Maintaining established Seed St pat, work to marker, bind off 5 sts (right armhole), continue in Seed St pat to next marker; turn and bind off 5 sts (left armhole), continue in Seed St pat back to right armhole—47 (55, 63, 71, 79) sts for back.

Work on back sts only; placing sts for fronts on holders.

Back
Bind off 4 sts at beg of next 2 rows—39 (47, 55, 63, 71) sts.

Work even in Seed St pat until armhole measures 5 (5½, 6, 7, 8) inches or desired length to shoulder, ending with a WS row.

Shape shoulders
Bind off 5 (6, 7, 9, 10) sts at beg of next 4 rows. Bind off rem 19 (23, 27, 27, 31) sts for back neck.

Left Front
Beg at armhole edge with RS facing, attach yarn and bind off 5 sts at beg of row, then 4 sts at beg of next RS row—20 (24, 28, 32, 36) sts.

Work 1 (1, 1, 3, 3) row(s) even in Seed St pat.

Shape V-neck
Maintaining established Seed St pat, dec 1 st at neck edge, by k2tog or p2tog, [every RS row] 10 (11, 12, 12, 13) times, then [every other RS row] 0 (1, 2, 2, 3) time(s)—10 (12, 14, 18, 20) sts.

Work even until same length as back, ending with a WS row.

Shape shoulder
Bind off 5 (6, 7, 9, 10) sts at armhole edge, work next row even, then bind off rem sts at armhole edge on last row.

Right Front
Beg at armhole edge with WS facing, attach yarn and bind off 5 sts at beg of row, then 4 sts at beg of next WS row—20 (24, 28, 32, 36) sts.

Work 2 (2, 2, 4, 4) rows even in Seed St pat.

Shape V-neck
Maintaining established Seed St pat, dec 1 st at neck edge, by ssk or ssp, [every RS row] 10 (11, 12, 12, 13) times, then [every other RS row] 0 (1, 2, 2, 3) time(s)—10 (12, 14, 18, 20) sts.

Work even until same length as back, ending with a RS row.

Shape shoulder
Bind off 5 (6, 7, 9, 10) sts at armhole edge, work next row even, then bind off rem sts at armhole edge on last row.

Assembly
Sew shoulder seams.

Armhole Edging
With RS facing, pick up and knit even around armhole, working approx 3 sts for every 4 rows and having an even number of sts; work in k1, p1 rib for ½ inch, or desired width. Bind off in pat.

Sew underarm seams, using first and last sts for seam.

Front Band
Mark placement of buttons on left front for girls and right front for boys.

With RS facing, pick up and knit evenly from lower right front, working approx 3 sts for every 4 rows and 1 st for each bound-off st across back neck, and then pick up and knit on left side to match right side, having an odd number of sts so bottom sts will match on fronts.

Work in k1, p1 rib for ¼ (¼, ¼, ½, ½) inch.

Work a 3-st buttonhole opposite each button marker. Work even for another ¼ inch. Bind off all sts in pat.

Sew buttons opposite buttonholes. ●

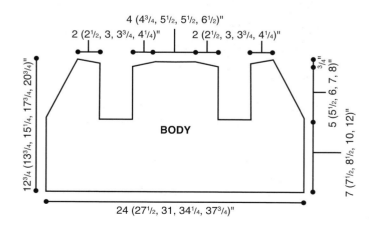

Baby Turtleback

You'll be amazed at how easy it is to make this clever design. Once you make one, you'll want to make them for everyone you love!

Design by Frances Hughes

Skill Level

■■□□ EASY

Sizes
Infant's size 0–6 (6–12, 12–18, 18–24) months
Instructions are given for smallest size, with larger sizes in parentheses. When only 1 number is given it applies to all sizes.

Finished Measurement
Approx 14 (16, 18, 20) inches square, before folding

Materials

- Sirdar Snuggly Baby Bamboo (DK weight; 80% bamboo/20% wool; 104 yds/50g per ball): 2 (2, 3, 3) balls coo #148
- Size 7 (4.5mm) 24-inch circular needle
- Size 10½ (6.5mm) 24-inch circular needle
- ⅔ yd 1½–2½-inch-wide ribbon (optional for closure)

Gauge
13 sts = 4 inches/10cm in St st on smaller needle.

Exact gauge is not critical to this project.

Pattern Stitch
Bluebell Rib (multiple of 5 sts + 2)
Row 1 (RS): P2, *k3, p2; rep from * across.
Rows 2 and 4: K2, *p3, k2; rep from * across.
Row 3: P2, *k3, p2; rep from * across.
Row 5: P2, *yo, sl 1, k2tog, psso, yo, p2; rep from * across.
Row 6: Rep Row 2.
Rep Rows 1–6 for pat.

Pattern Notes
Piece is worked as a square, and then folded and sewn at the sides, leaving openings for armholes.

When worn, the looseness of the rib pattern tends to cause the piece to "grow" in width for a flexible fit.

When measuring length of the piece, be sure to do so with piece on a flat surface.

Turtleback
With larger needle, loosely cast on 82 (92, 102, 112) sts.

Rep [Rows 1–6 of Bluebell Rib pat] 1 (1, 2, 2) time(s).

Change to smaller needle and continue in pat until piece measures 12 (14, 16, 18) inches from cast-on edge, ending by working a Row 6 of pat.

Change to larger needle and work [Rows 1–6] 2 (2, 3, 3) times.

Bind off loosely.

Finishing
Referring to diagram, fold piece in half matching cast-on and bound-off larger-needle edges. Mark sides 3 (3½, 4, 4½) inches from fold for armhole openings. Sew side seams tog joining area 3 to area 2 and area 4 to area 1 from marker to lower edge.

Referring to photo, weave ribbon between sts on each side and tie at center front.

When worn, 1 large-needle end becomes the collar and the other becomes the flounce. ●

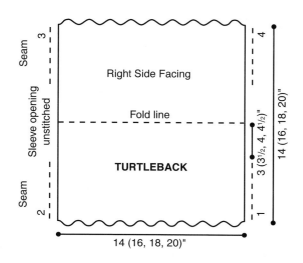

House of White Birches, Berne, Indiana 46711   AnniesAttic.com   **85**

Curvy Cabled Scarf

The scarf undulates with the curves of the cables.

Design by Suzanne Atkinson

Skill Level
■■■□ INTERMEDIATE

Finished Size
Approx 5 x 62 inches

Materials
- Plymouth Galway Chunky (bulky weight; 100% wool; 123 yds/100g per ball): 2 balls purple #13
- Size 10 (6mm) needles or size needed to obtain gauge
- Cable needle

5 BULKY

Gauge
30 sts = 5 inches/12.5cm and 24 rows = 4¾ inches in Cable Pat.

Exact gauge is not critical to this project.

Special Abbreviations
Twist 3 Back (T3B): Slip next st to cn, hold in back, k2, p1 from cn.

Twist 3 Front (T3F): Slip next 2 sts to cn, hold in front, p1, k2 from cn.

Cable 4 Back (C4B): Slip next 2 sts to cn, hold in back, k2, k2 from cn.

Cable 4 Front (C4F): Slip next 2 sts to cn, hold in front, k2, k2 from cn.

Increase (inc): Inc by knitting in front and back of next st.

Pattern Stitch
Note: A chart is provided for those preferring to work Cable pat from a chart.

Cable
Row 1 (RS): Sl 1, p1, [T3B, T3F] 3 times, p1, k1.
Row 2: Sl 1, inc, p2, [k2, p4] twice, k2, p2, inc, k1—24 sts.

Row 3: Sl 1, p1, T3B, [p2, C4B] twice, p2, T3F, p1, k1.
Row 4: Sl 1, inc, p2, k3, p4, k2, p4, k3, p2, inc, k1—26 sts.
Row 5: Sl 1, p1, T3B, p2, [T3B, T3F] twice, p2, T3F, p1, k1.
Row 6: Sl 1, inc, p2, k3, p2, k2, p4, k2, p2, k3, p2, inc 1, k1—28 sts.
Row 7: Sl 1, p1, [T3B, p2] twice, C4F, [p2, T3F] twice, p1, k1.
Row 8: Sl 1, inc, [p2, k3] twice, p4, [k3, p2] twice, inc, k1—30 sts.
Row 9: Sl 1, p1, [T3B, p2] twice, T3B, [T3F, p2] twice, T3F, p1, k1.
Row 10: Sl 1, k1, [p2, k3] twice, p2, k2, [p2, k3] twice, p2, k2.
Row 11: Sl 1, p1, [k2, p3] twice, k2, p2, [k2, p3] twice, k2, p1, k1.
Row 12: Sl 1, k1, [p2, k3] twice, p2, k2, [p2, k3] twice, p2, k2.
Row 13: Sl 1, p1, [T3F, p2] twice, T3F, [T3B, p2] twice, T3B, p1, k1.
Row 14: Sl 1, ssk, [p2, k3] twice, p4, [k3, p2] twice, k2tog, k1—28 sts.
Row 15: Sl 1, p1, [T3F, p2] twice, C4F, [p2, T3B] twice, p1, k1.
Row 16: Sl 1, ssk, p2, k3, p2, k2, p4, k2, p2, k3, p2, k2tog, k1—26 sts.
Row 17: Sl 1, p1, T3F, p2, [T3F, T3B] twice, p2, T3B, p1, k1.
Row 18: Sl 1, ssk, p2, k3, p4, k2, p4, k3, p2, k2tog, k1—24 sts.
Row 19: Sl 1, p1, T3F, [p2, C4B] twice, p2, T3B, p1, k1.
Row 20: Sl 1, ssk, p2, [k2, p4] twice, k2, p2, k2tog, k1—22 sts.
Row 21: Sl 1, p1, [T3F, T3B] 3 times, p1, k1.
Row 22: Sl 1, k2, [p4, k2] twice, p4, k3.
Row 23: Sl 1, [p2, C4F] 3 times, p2, k1.
Row 24: Sl 1, [k2, p4] 3 times, k3.
Rep Rows 1–24 for Cable pat.

Pattern Notes

Slip first st of every row purlwise with yarn in front.

Outer edges of scarf are shaped with increases and decreases. The stitch count varies throughout the pattern; the cable begins on 22 stitches, increases on wrong-side rows to 30 stitches, then decreases on wrong-side rows back to 22 stitches.

Scarf

Cast on 22 sts.

Set-up row (WS): Work Row 24 of Cable pat.

Work [Rows 1–24 of Cable pat] 12 times, then rep [Rows 1–21] once.

Bind off in pat on Row 22, dec 3 sts evenly across row while binding off.

Block to measurements. ●

STITCH KEY
- ☐ K on RS, p on WS
- ⊟ P on RS, k on WS
- V Sl 1 pwise wyif
- Y Inc 1
- ◣ Ssk
- ◿ K2tog
- T3B
- T3F
- C4B
- C4F

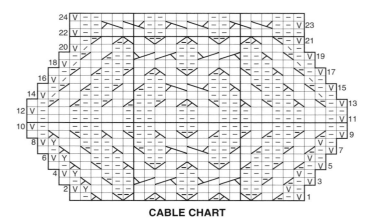

CABLE CHART

Crisscross Cable Shrug

Choose a vibrant shade for this knit-in-the-round cozy.

Design by Kathy Wesley

Skill Level
■■□□ EASY

Size
Woman's small (medium, large) Instructions are given for smallest size, with larger sizes in parentheses. When only 1 number is given, it applies to all sizes.

Finished Measurement
Circumference: Approx 25½ (27¼, 29) inches
Note: Due to rib pat, shrug has significant amount of stretch.

Materials
- Worsted weight yarn (175 yds/ 100g per ball): 2 (2, 3) balls pink
- Size 9 (5.5mm) circular needle or size needed to obtain gauge
- Cable needle
- Stitch marker

MEDIUM

Gauge
22 sts = 4 inches/10cm in pat.

To save time, take time to check gauge.

Special Abbreviation
Cable Back (CB): Slip next 2 sts to cn and hold in back, k2, k2 from cn.

Pattern Stitch
Crisscross Cable (multiple of 10 sts)
Rnd 1: *P1, k4, p2, k2, p1; rep from * around.
Rnds 2–4: Rep Rnd 1.
Rnd 5: *P1, CB, p2, k2, p1; rep from * around.
Rnds 6–8: Rep Rnd 1.
Rnd 9: *P2, k2, p2, k4; rep from * around.
Rnds 10–12: Rep Rnd 9.
Rnd 13: *P2, k2, p2, CB; rep from * around.
Rnds 14–16: Rep Rnd 13.
Rep Rnds 1–16 for pat.

Shrug
Cast on 140 (152, 160) sts. Mark beg of rnd and join without twisting.

Rnd 1: *P2, k2; rep from * around.

Rnds 2 and 3: Rep Rnd 1.

Rnd 4: Rep Rnd 1, dec by k2tog 0 (2, 0) sts evenly around—140 (150, 160) sts.

Work [Rnds 1–16 of Crisscross Cable pat] 4 times, then rep Rnds 1–4 once.

Bind off in pat. ●

Send a Little Cable

Keep winter's chill away in style—no cable needle required!

Design by Amy Polcyn

Skill Level
◼◼◼◻ INTERMEDIATE

Size
Adult's

Finished Measurement
Foot circumference: 8 inches

Materials
- SWTC Karaoke (worsted weight; 50% soy silk/50% wool; 110 yds/ 50g per ball): 2 balls red #512
- Size 6 (4mm) double-point needles or size needed to obtain gauge
- Stitch holder
- Stitch marker

4 MEDIUM

Gauge
20 sts and 28 rows = 4 inches/10cm in pat.

To save time, take time to check gauge.

Special Abbreviations
N1, N2, N3, N4: Needle 1, Needle 2, Needle 3, Needle 4.

Pattern Stitch
Baby Cable (multiple of 4 sts)
Rnds 1–3: *K2, p2; rep from * around.
Rnd 4: *K2tog, leave sts on LH needle, insert tip of RH needle back into first st, k1, sl sts off needle, p2; rep from * around.
Rep Rnds 1–4 for pat.

Pattern Note
Slip all stitches purlwise.

Leg
Cast on 40 sts, divide on dpn, place marker for beg of rnd and join without twisting.

Work in Baby Cable pat for 4 inches, ending with Rnd 4 of pat.

Heel flap
K8, turn. P18. These sts will form heel flap. Place rem 22 instep sts on holder. Heel flap is worked back and forth in rows.

Row 1: *Sl 1, k1; rep from * across.

Row 2: Sl 1, purl across.

Rows 3–18: Rep Rows 1 and 2.

There will be 9 edge-chain sts along each side of heel flap.

Heel turn
Row 1: K11, ssk, k1, turn.

Row 2: Sl 1, p5, p2tog, p1, turn.

Row 3: Sl 1, knit to 1 st before gap, ssk (taking 1 st from each side of gap), k1, turn.

Row 4: Sl 1, purl to 1 st before gap, p2tog (taking 1 st from each side of gap), p1, turn.

Rep Rows 3 and 4 until all heel sts have been worked, ending with a WS row—2 sts.

Gusset
Set-up rnd: N1: knit across 12 heel sts, pick up and knit 9 sts along side of heel flap; N2: work 22 instep sts in pat; N3: pick up and knit 9 sts along other side of heel flap, knit across 6 heel sts from N1; mark center back heel as beg of rnd—52 sts.

Rnd 1: N1: knit to last 3 sts, k2tog, k1; N2: work instep sts; N3: k1, ssk, knit to end.

Rnd 2: Work even in established pat.

Rep Rnds 1 and 2 until 40 sts rem.

Foot
Work even in pat until foot measures approx 2 inches less than desired length.

Toe

Change to St st.

Rnd 1: N1: knit to last 3 sts, k2tog, k1; N2: k1, ssk, knit to last 3 sts, k2tog, k1; N3: k1, ssk, knit to end.

Rnd 2: Knit around.

Rep Rnds 1 and 2 until 8 sts rem.

Divide sts evenly between 2 needles. Weave toe sts tog using Kitchener st, page 122. ●

On a Roll Doll Cardigan

Both she and her doll will love this colorful and fun little playtime sweater.

Design by Erli Gronberg

Skill Level
■■■□ INTERMEDIATE

Finished Size
Fits 18-inch doll

Materials

- Universal Poems Sock (sock weight; 75% superwash wool/25% nylon; 459 yds/100g per skein): 1 skein tropical sunset #955 (MC)
- Universal Pace (sock weight; 75% superwash wool/25% nylon; 220 yds/50g per skein): 1 skein persimmon #09 (CC)
- Size 3 (3.25mm) needles or size needed to obtain gauge
- 5 (½-inch) buttons

Gauge
14 sts and 20 rows = 2 inches in St st.

To save time, take time to check gauge.

Special Abbreviation
Increase (inc): Inc by knitting into front and back of next st.

Back
With MC, cast on 52 sts and work in k2, p2 rib for ¾ inch.

Beg pat
Rows 1–4: Beg with a RS row and MC, work in St st.

Rows 5–10: With CC, work in St st.

Row 11 (RS): Change to MC; *with tip of RH needle, pick up CC loop from WS 6 rows below, put on LH needle, k2tog; rep from * across to form roll or tuck.

Rows 12–14: With MC, work in St st.

Rows 15–22: With CC, work in St st.

Row 23: Change to MC; *with tip RH needle, pick up CC loop from WS 8 rows below, put on LH needle, k2tog; rep from * across.

Continue with MC in St st until back measures 3¼ inches from beg.

Shape armhole
Bind off 3 sts at beg of next 4 rows—40 sts.

Continue even in St st until back measures 5¾ inches from beg, ending with a WS row.

Right shoulder
Row 1 (RS): K16, turn, leaving rem sts on needle.

Row 2: Bind off 3 sts, purl across—13 sts.

Row 3: Knit across.

Rows 4 and 5: Rep Rows 2 and 3—10 sts.

Bind off 10 sts.

Left shoulder
Row 1 (RS): Join yarn at neck edge, bind off center 8 sts, knit across—16 sts.

Row 2: Purl across.

Row 3: Bind off 3 sts, knit across—13 sts.

Rows 4 and 5: Rep Rows 2 and 3—10 sts.

Bind off 10 sts.

Left Front
With MC, cast on 24 sts. Work as for back until front measures 3¼ inches from beg, ending with a WS row.

Shape armhole
At beg of RS row, bind off [3 sts] twice—18 sts.

Continue even in St st until front measures 5½ inches from beg, ending with a RS row.

Shape neck

At beg of WS row bind off [3 sts] twice, then [2 sts] once—10 sts.

Next row (RS): Knit across.

Bind off all sts.

Right Front

Work as for left front, until front measures 3¼ inches from beg, ending with a RS row.

Shape armhole

At beg of WS row bind off [3 sts] twice—18 sts.

Continue even in St st until front measures 5½ inches from beg, ending with a WS row.

Shape neck

At beg of RS row bind off [3 sts] twice, then [2 sts] once—10 sts.

Bind off all sts.

Sleeves

With MC, cast on 28 sts, work in k2, p2 rib for ¾ inch, inc 1 st at each end of last row—30 sts.

Beg pat

Rows 1–4: With MC, work in St st, inc 1 st at each edge on Row 3—32 sts.

Rows 5–10: With CC, work in St st.

Row 11 (RS): Change to MC; *with tip of RH needle, pick up CC loop from WS 6 rows below, put on LH needle, k2tog; rep from * across, forming roll.

Rows 12–14: With MC, work in St st, inc 1 st at each edge on Row 13—34 sts.

Rows 15–22: With CC, work in St st.

Row 23: Change to MC; *with tip RH needle, pick up CC loop from WS 8 rows below, put on LH needle, k2tog; rep from * across.

With MC, work in St st, inc 1 st at each edge [every 4th row] until there are 38 sts, then work even as needed until sleeve measures 3¼ inches from beg.

Shape cap

Bind off 3 sts at beg of next 4 rows—26 sts.

Bind off 1 st at beg of next 10 rows—16 sts

Bind off 2 sts at beg of next 4 rows—8 sts.

Note: Sleeve should measure approx 5½ inches from beg.

Bind off all sts.

Assembly

Sew shoulder seams.

Sew sleeves in armholes, and then sew side and sleeve seams, leaving rolls separate. Join ends of rolls tog at seams.

Neckband

With MC and RS facing, pick up and knit 8 sts along right front neck, 24 sts across back, and 8 sts along left front neck—40 sts.

Work in k2, p2 rib until band measures ¾ inch. Bind off in pat.

Button Band

With MC and RS facing, pick up and knit 48 sts along left front edge, picking up sts through rolls.

Work in k2, p2 rib for 5 rows. Bind off in pat.

Buttonhole Band

With MC and RS facing, pick up and knit 48 sts along right front edge, picking up sts through rolls.

Row 1 (WS): Work in k2, p2 rib.

Row 2 (buttonhole row): K2, [yo, p2tog, work 8 sts in established rib] 4 times, end yo, p2tog, k2, p2.

Rows 3–5: Work in k2, p2 rib.

Bind off in pat.

Sew buttons opposite buttonholes. ●

Bobble-Edged Cardigan

Tiny bobbles push the cute factor over the edge!

Design by Kathy Disantis and Dianne Rodabaugh for Ewe & I Originals

Skill Level

 INTERMEDIATE

Sizes

Child's size 2 (4, 6) Instructions are given for smallest size, with larger sizes in parentheses. When only 1 number is given, it applies to all sizes.

Finished Measurements

Chest: 24 (26½, 29¼) inches
Length: 10½ (13, 15½) inches

Materials

- Malabrigo Merino Worsted (worsted weight; 100% wool; 210 yds/100g per skein): 2 (2, 3) skeins Melilla #226
- Size 9 (5.5mm) 24-inch circular needle
- Size 10 (6mm) needles or size needed to obtain gauge
- Stitch markers
- Stitch holders
- 3 (1⅛-inch) buttons

Gauge

18 sts and 24 rows = 4 inches/10cm in St st with larger needles.

To save time, take time to check gauge.

Special Abbreviations

Make Bobble (MB): In next st, work [k1, p1] twice, turn; p4, turn; k4, turn; [p2tog] twice, turn; k2tog—1 st rem.

Increase (inc): Inc by making a backward loop on RH needle.

Pattern Stitches

Bobble Edge (multiple of 6 sts + 5)
Row 1 (WS): Knit across.
Row 2: K2, *MB, k5; rep from * across to last 3 sts, end MB, k2.

Checkerboard (multiple of 12 sts)
Rows 1, 3, 5 and 7: *P6, k6; rep from * across.
Rows 2, 4, 6 and 8: *K6, p6; rep from * across.
Rows 9, 11, 13 and 15: *K6, p6; rep from * across.
Rows 10, 12, 14 and 16: *P6, k6; rep from * across.
Rep Rows 1–16 for pat.

Pattern Note

Work decreases 1 stitch in from each edge on right-side rows using slip, slip, knit (ssk) decrease at the beginning of the row, and knit 2 together (k2tog) decrease at the end of the row.

Back

With larger needles cast on 53 (59, 65) sts.

Work Rows 1 and 2 of Bobble Edge pat.

Work in garter st for 5 (7, 9) rows, inc 1 st on last row—54 (60, 66) sts.

Set up pat

Row 1 (RS): Work Row 1 of Checkerboard pat to last 6 (0, 6) sts, end p6 (0, 6).

Work in established pat until back measures 6 (7½, 9) inches from beg.

Shape armholes

Maintaining pat, bind off 2 (2, 3) sts at beg of next 2 rows—50 (56, 60) sts.

Continue to work in pat until back measures 10 (12½, 15) inches from beg. Mark center 16 (18, 20) sts.

Shape shoulders

Work to first marker, bind off center 16 (18, 20) sts; attach 2nd ball of yarn and complete row.

Working both sides at once with separate balls of yarn, dec 1 st at each neck edge—16 (18, 19) shoulder sts.

Continue in pat until back measures 10½ (13, 15½) inches. Place shoulder sts on holders.

Left Front

With larger needles cast on 29 (29, 35) sts.

Work Rows 1 and 2 of Bobble Edge pat.

Work in garter st for 5 (7, 9) rows, inc 1 st on last row—30 (30, 36) sts.

Set up pat

Row 1 (RS): Work Row 1 of Checkerboard pat to last 6 (6, 0) sts, end p6 (6, 0).

Work in established pat until front measures 6 (7½, 9) inches from beg, ending with a WS row.

Shape armhole

Bind off 2 (2, 3) sts at beg of row, and *at the same time*, dec 1 st at neck edge [every RS row] 12 (10, 14) times—16 (18, 19) sts.

Continue in pat until front measures 10½ (13, 15½) inches. Place rem sts on holder.

Right Front

Work as for left front to armhole shaping, ending with a RS row.

Bind off 2 (2, 3) sts at beg of row, and *at the same time*, dec 1 st at neck edge [every RS row] 12 (10, 14) times—16 (18, 19) sts.

Continue to work in pat until front measures 10½ (13, 15½) inches. Place rem sts on holder.

Sleeves

With larger needles, cast on 29 (29, 35) sts.

Work Rows 1 and 2 of Bobble Edge pat.

Work in garter st for 5 (7, 9) rows, inc 1 st on last row—30 (30, 36) sts.

Set up pat

Row 1 (RS): Work Row 1 of Checkerboard pat to last 6 (6, 0) sts, end p6 (6, 0).

Work in pat, inc 1 st at each edge [every other row] 0 (2, 0) times, [every 4th row] 0 (8, 11) times, then [every 5th row] 6 (0, 0) times, working new sts into pat—42 (50, 58) sts.

Continue in pat until sleeve measures 7 (9, 11) inches from beg. Bind off all sts.

Assembly

Join front and back shoulders, using 3-Needle Bind-Off, page 122.

Sew sleeves to body, sew side and sleeve seams.

Front Band

With smaller circular needle and RS facing, beg at lower right front edge. Pick up and knit 30 (38, 46) sts to first neck dec, 21 (26, 30) sts along neck edge, 22 (24, 26) sts across back neck, 21 (26, 30) sts along left neck edge, and 30 (38, 46) sts to lower left edge—124 (152, 178) sts.

Work in garter st for ½ inch. On next row, work 3 buttonholes evenly spaced from bottom edge to beg of V-neck, by binding off 4 sts for each button-hole on the next row and casting on 4 sts over each buttonhole on the following row. Continue to work in garter st until band measures approx 1 inch, ending with a WS row. Bind off all sts.

Sew buttons opposite buttonholes. ●

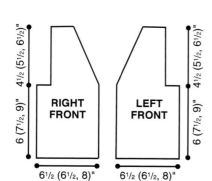

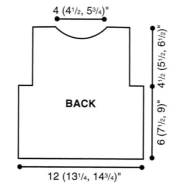

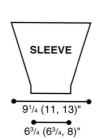

Lace Socks

Delicate lace knits up quickly in these summertime socks.

Design by DROPS Design for Garnstudio

Skill Level

■■■■ EXPERIENCED

Sizes

Fits woman's shoe sizes 5/6 (7/8½, 10/12) Instructions are given for smallest size, with larger sizes in parentheses. When only 1 number is given, it applies to all sizes.

Finished Measurement

Foot length: Approx 8⅝ (9½, 10⅝) inches

Materials

- Garnstudio DROPS Alpaca (sport weight; 100% alpaca; 182 yards/ 50g per ball): 2 balls white #1101
- Size 4 (3.5mm) set of double-point needles or size needed to obtain gauge
- Size D/3 (3.25mm) crochet hook
- Stitch markers
- Stitch holders

Gauge

23 sts and 30 rows = 4 inches/10cm in St st.

To save time, take time to check gauge.

Special Abbreviation

Slip, slip, purl (ssp): Slip next 2 sts 1 at a time kwise from LH to RH needle; slip sts back to LH needle keeping them twisted, p2tog-tbl.

Pattern Stitch

Work according to charts.

Sock

With dpns, cast on 49 (49, 57) sts. Place marker on needle for center back and join without twisting.

Knit 2 rnds.

Set up pat

Rnds 1–24: Work Rnds 1–24 of Chart A (approx 3½ inches).

Keep first 12 (12, 16) sts on needle, slip next 25 sts on a holder for instep, keep last 12 (12, 16) sts on needle (yarn will be at center back).

Divide for heel

With needle containing last 12 (12, 16) sts, knit across first needle—24 (24, 32) sts for heel.

Work back and forth in St st over heel sts for 2 (2¼, 2½) inches. Mark this row and measure foot length from here.

Shape heel

Row 1 (RS): Knit to last 7 (7, 9) sts, ssk, turn.

Row 2: Purl to last 7 (7, 9) sts, ssp, turn.

Row 3: Knit to last 6 (6, 8) sts, ssk, turn.

Row 4: Purl to last 6 (6, 8) sts, ssp, turn.

Continue to work short rows in this manner, with 1 st less at end of row, until 12 (12, 16) sts rem.

Foot

Pick up and knit 12 (12, 14) sts along edge of heel flap, work in established pat across 25 instep sts from holder, pick up and knit 12 (12, 14) sts along edge of heel flap—61 (61, 69) sts.

Join and work foot in St st and 25 instep sts in lace pat as follows:

Sizes 5/6 (7/8½): Work pat from Chart B.
Size 10/12: Work pat from Chart A, beg and ending as shown, and working rep twice.

At the same time, dec 1 st at each side by working ssk on last 2 sts before lace panel, and k2tog on first 2 sts after lace panel. Work dec [every other rnd] 7 (5, 7) times—47 (51, 55) sts.

Continue in St st and established lace pat until foot measures 7 (8, 9) inches from marker at heel, knit 1 rnd over all sts, dec 1 st—46 (50, 54) sts.

Place a marker after 23rd (25th, 27th) st—23 (25, 27) sts between markers.

Toe

Dec rnd: [Knit to 2 sts before marker, k2tog, slip marker, ssk] twice, knit to end.

Next rnd: Knit around.

Work Dec rnd [every other rnd] 3 times, then [every rnd] 7 times—6 (10, 14) sts rem.

Next rnd: K2tog around.

Cut yarn, pull through rem sts, pull tight and fasten off securely.

Crocheted Edge

Note: If not familiar with single crochet (sc) st, see illustration on page 122.

Crochet around cast-on edge: Join with sc in first cast-on st, *ch 4, sc in 2nd ch, skip approx ½ inch on edge, sc in the next st; rep from * around entire top edge of sock, finish with sl st in first sc. ●

STITCH KEY
☐ Knit
⊙ Yo
╱ K2tog
╲ Ssk
⅄ Sl 1, k2tog, psso

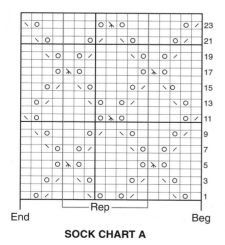

SOCK CHART A

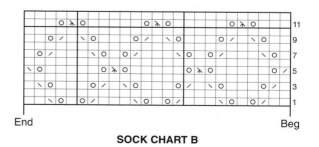

SOCK CHART B

Cat's-Eye Scarf or Belt

Wear it as a belt, wear it as a scarf. Either way you can't go wrong.

Design by Kathy Wesley

Skill Level
⬛⬛◻◻ EASY

Finished Size
Approx 4 x 68 inches

Materials
- Patons Grace (DK weight; 100% cotton; 136 yds/50g per ball): 2 balls viola #62322
- Size 5 (3.75mm) needles or size needed to obtain gauge

3 LIGHT

Gauge
20 sts = 4 inches/10cm in Cat's-Eye pat.

To save time, take time to check gauge.

Special Abbreviation
Double yarn over (2yo): Wrap yarn twice around needle. On next row, p1, k1 in 2yo.

Pattern Stitch
Cat's-Eye (multiple of 4 sts)
Row 1: K4, *2yo, k4; rep from * across.
Row 2: K1, p1, *p2tog, [p1, k1] in 2yo of previous row, p2tog; rep from * to last 2 sts, p1, k1.
Row 3: K2, yo, *k4, 2yo; rep from * to last 6 sts, k4, yo, k2.
Row 4: K1, p2, *[p2tog] twice, [p1, k1] in 2yo of previous row; rep from * to last 7 sts, [p2tog] twice, p2, k1.
Rep Rows 1–4 for pat.

Belt/Scarf
Cast on 20 sts. Purl 1 row.

Work Rows 1–4 of Cat's-Eye pat until belt/scarf measures approx 68 inches.
Bind off. ●

House of White Birches, Berne, Indiana 46711   AnniesAttic.com

Ridged Moebius

Made with bulky-weight yarn, there's no reason why you can't whip this ultra-stylish moebius up today!

Design by Zena Low

Skill Level

■■■□ INTERMEDIATE

Finished Size
Approx 40 x 14 inches

Materials
- Bulky weight yarn (72% acrylic/28% polyester): 160 yds pale blue
- Size 15 (10mm) 36-inch circular needle or size needed to obtain gauge
- Stitch marker

5 BULKY

Gauge
10 sts and 12 rows = 4 inches/10cm in St st.

To save time, take time to check gauge.

Pattern Note
To create the twist in the moebius, turn the first 3 or 4 sts on the left-hand needle completely around the needle before joining to work the first round.

Wrap
Cast on 90 sts. Place marker on needle, twist first 3 or 4 stitches on LH needle completely around needle; place marker on needle and join to work in rnds.

Rnds 1–8: Knit around.

Rnds 9–16: Purl around.

Rnds 17–22: Knit around.

Rnds 23–27: Purl around.

Rnds 28–32: Knit around.

Rnds 33–40: Purl around.

Bind off all sts pwise. ●

Everything Good
Comes in Threes (or More!)

If garments are what you seek, this chapter gives you even more reason to dive into

your stash. On the pages that follow, you'll find projects to make those skeins stretch

even further. We bring you some eye-catching garments, such as sleeveless tunics and

tanks that are perfect for layering, calling for three, four, five or six balls or skeins.

Flirty Top

With doubled yarn above and single below, this demure top will seduce you!

Design by Ann E. Smith

Skill Level

■■■□ INTERMEDIATE

Sizes

Woman's extra-small (small, medium, large, extra-large, 2X-large) Instructions are given for smallest size, with larger sizes in parentheses. When only 1 number is given, it applies to all sizes.

Finished Measurements

Chest: 30 (34, 38, 42, 46, 50½) inches
Length: 19 (19½, 20, 20½, 21, 21½) inches

Materials

- Berroco Seduce (worsted weight; 47% rayon/25% linen/17% silk/ 11% nylon; 100 yds/40g per hank): 4 (5, 6, 6, 7, 8) hanks earth stone #4430 (A) and 2 (3, 3, 3, 4, 4) hanks gris-bleu #4437 (B) **4 MEDIUM**
- Size 7 (4.5mm) straight and 16-inch circular needles or size needed to obtain gauge
- Stitch markers

Gauge

18 sts and 24 rows = 4 inches/10cm in Lace pat with single strand.

15½ sts and 23 rows = 4 inches/10cm in St st with 1 strand of each A and B held tog.

To save time, take time to check gauge.

Pattern Stitches

Lace Back (multiple of 6 sts + 3)
Row 1 and all WS rows: Purl across.
Rows 2 (RS), 4 and 6: K2, *yo, ssk, k1, k2tog, yo, k1; rep from * across to last st, end k1.
Row 8: K3, *yo, sl 1, k2tog, psso, yo, k3; rep from * across.
Row 10: K2, *k2tog, yo, k1, yo, ssk, k1; rep from * across to last st, end k1.

Row 12: K1, k2tog, *yo, k3, yo, sl 1, k2tog, psso; rep from * to last 6 sts, end yo, k3, yo, ssk, k1.
Rep Rows 1–12 for Lace Back pat.

Lace Front (multiple of 6 sts + 3)
Row 1 and all WS rows: Purl across.
Rows 2 (RS), 4 and 6: K2, *k2tog, yo, k1, yo, ssk, k1; rep from * across to last st, end k1.
Row 8: K1, k2tog, *yo, k3, yo, sl 1, k2tog, psso; rep from * to last 6 sts, end yo, k3, yo, ssk, k1.
Row 10: K2, *yo, ssk, k1, k2tog, yo, k1; rep from * across to last st, end k1.
Row 12: K3, *yo, sl 1, k2tog, psso, yo, k3; rep from * across.
Rep Rows 1–12 for Lace Front pat.

Pattern Notes

Work decreases 1 stitch in from each edge on right-side rows using slip, slip, knit (ssk) decrease at the beginning of the row, and knit 2 together (k2tog) decrease at the end of the row.

Back

With A, cast on 87 (99, 111, 123, 135, 147) sts. Work [Rows 1–12 of Lace Back pat] 4 times.

Next row: [P1, p2tog] across—58 (66, 74, 82, 90, 98) sts.

Bodice

With 1 strand each of A and B held tog, beg with a knit row, work in St st until bodice measures 4 inches, ending with a WS row.

Shape armholes

Bind off 4 (4, 4, 5, 6, 7) sts at beg of next 2 rows, then dec 1 st at each edge [every RS row] 2 (4, 6, 7, 8, 9) times—46 (50, 54, 58, 62, 66) sts.

Work even until bodice measures 11 (11½, 12, 12½, 13, 13½) inches, ending with a WS row. Bind off all sts.

Front

With A, cast on 87 (99, 111, 123, 135, 147) sts. Work [Rows 1–12 of Lace Front pat] 4 times.

Next row: [P1, p2tog] across—58 (66, 74, 82, 90, 98) sts.

Bodice

With 1 strand each of A and B held tog, beg with a knit row, work in St st until bodice measures 4 inches, ending with a WS row.

Shape armholes

Bind off 4 (4, 4, 5, 6, 7) sts at beg of next 2 rows, then dec 1 st at each edge [every RS row] 2 (4, 6, 7, 8, 9) times, and *at the same time,* when bodice measures 5¾ (6¼, 6¾, 7¼, 7¾, 8¼) inches from beg, end with a WS row. Place markers on each side of center 22 (22, 24, 26, 28, 30) sts.

Shape neck

Knit across to marker, bind off center 22 (22, 24, 25, 28, 30) sts, knit to end.

Shape right shoulder

Next row (WS): Purl across.

Bind off at beg of RS row [3 sts] once, [2 sts] once, and [1 st] once—6 (8, 9, 10, 11, 12) sts.

Work even until armhole measures same as back to shoulder, ending with a RS row.

Bind off all sts.

Shape left shoulder

At beg of WS rows, with 1 strand each of A and B held tog, bind off [3 sts] once, [2 sts] once, and [1 st] once—6 (8, 9, 10, 11, 12) sts.

Work even until armhole measures same as back to shoulder, ending with a WS row.

Bind off all sts.

Assembly

Sew shoulder seams.

Finishing

Armbands

With RS facing and 1 strand each of A and B held tog, pick up and knit 68 (74, 78, 84, 88, 94) sts around armhole opening.

Knit 2 rows. Bind off kwise on WS.

Rep for other armband.

Neckband

With RS facing and 1 strand each of A and B held tog and beg at center front with circular needle, pick up and knit 11 (11, 12, 13, 14, 15) sts across front neck, 27 sts along side of neck, 34 (34, 36, 38, 40, 42) sts across back neck, 27 sts along side of neck, and 11 (11, 12, 13, 14, 15) sts to center front—110 (110, 114, 118, 122, 126) sts.

Knit 4 rows.

Bind off kwise on WS.

Sew side seams.

Tie

With 1 strand each of A and B held tog, cast on 2 sts.

Knit every row until tie measures 38 (42, 46, 50, 54, 58) inches from beg. Bind off. Secure ends.

Beg and ending at center front, weave tie through last row of eyelets. Try on garment. With ends of tie even, tighten to fit snugly to body and tie. Twist ends until they begin to curl. Let curl form a rosette. Take ends from front to back through center and tuck in place. ●

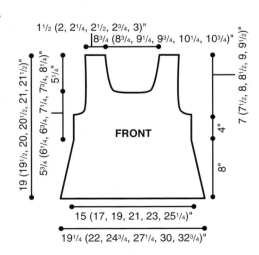

1½ (2, 2¼, 2½, 2¾, 3)"
8¾ (8¾, 9¼, 9¾, 10¼, 10¾)"
7 (7½, 8, 8½, 9, 9½)"
19 (19½, 20, 20½, 21, 21½)"
5¾ (6¼, 6¾, 7¼, 7¾, 8¼)"
5¼"
4"
8"
FRONT
15 (17, 19, 21, 23, 25¼)"
19¼ (22, 24¾, 27¼, 30, 32¾)"

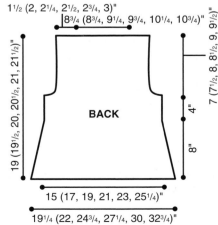

1½ (2, 2¼, 2½, 2¾, 3)"
8¾ (8¾, 9¼, 9¾, 10¼, 10¾)"
7 (7½, 8, 8½, 9, 9½)"
19 (19½, 20, 20½, 21, 21½)"
4"
8"
BACK
15 (17, 19, 21, 23, 25¼)"
19¼ (22, 24¾, 27¼, 30, 32¾)"

Splendiferous

As delicate as a whisper on a breeze, layer this over a dress or pants.

Design by Cheryl Beckerich

Skill Level
■■■□ INTERMEDIATE

Sizes
Woman's small (medium, large, extra-large, 2X-large) Instructions are given for smallest size, with larger sizes in parentheses. When only 1 number is given, it applies to all sizes.

Finished Measurements
Chest: 38 (42, 46, 50, 54) inches
Length: 33 (33, 33, 34, 34) inches

Materials
- Scarlet Fleece Grassy Wool (fingering weight; 65% superwash merino wool/35% bamboo; 429 yds/3 oz per skein): 2 (3, 3, 3, 3) skeins under the sea colorway
- Size 6 (4mm) 16- inch and 29-inch circular needles or size needed to obtain gauge
- Stitch markers
- Stitch holders

Gauge
19 sts and 24 rows = 4 inches/10cm in pat.

To save time, take time to check gauge.

Pattern Stitches
Lace (multiple of 8 sts; worked in rnds)
Rnds 1 and 3: Knit around.
Rnd 2: *K2tog, yo, k3, yo, ssk, k1; rep from * around.
Rnd 4: *K2, yo, sk2p, yo, k3; rep from * around.
Rep Rnds 1–4 for pat.

Lace (multiple of 8 sts; worked in rows)
Rows 1 and 3 (WS): Purl across.
Row 2: *K2tog, yo, k3, yo, ssk, k1; rep from * across.
Row 4: *K2, yo, sk2p, yo, k3; rep from * across.
Rep Rows 1–4 for pat.

Pattern Notes
Garment is worked in the round from lower edge to armholes, and then divided to work fronts and back separately in rows.

To ensure even distribution of color, alternately work 2 rows from 2 different skeins of yarn. Take care to change skeins at the side, not at the front of garment.

Work decreases as slip, slip, knit (ssk) after markers at beginning of right-side rows and as knit 2 together (k2tog) before markers/at end of right-side rows. Work decreases as purl 2 together (p2tog) at beginning of wrong-side rows and slip, slip, purl (ssp) at end of wrong-side rows. When shaping armholes and neck, work decreases 1 stitch from edge, maintaining edge stitch in stockinette stitch.

When working shaping in Lace pattern, if there are not enough stitches, work a decrease with its accompanying yarn over, work stitches in stockinette stitch.

Body
With longer needle, cast on 96 (112, 120, 128, 136) sts, place marker, cast on 96 (112, 120, 128, 136) sts—192 (224, 240, 256, 272) sts.

Place marker for beg of rnd, and join without twisting.

Work 5 rnds in St st.

Beg Lace pat in rnds and work even until body measures 2 (2, 2, 3, 3) inches from beg.

Shape waist
Beg on next rnd, dec 1 st before and after each marker [every 16 rnds] 4 (4, 4, 5, 5) times, then [every 12 rnds] 3 (3, 3, 2, 2) times—164 (196, 212, 228, 244) sts.

Work even in pat for 1 inch.

Shape bust
Beg on next rnd, inc 1 st before and after each marker [every 10 (10, 9, 9, 9) rnds 7 times—192 (224, 240, 256, 272) sts.

Work even as needed until body measures 26 (25½, 25, 25¾, 25¼) inches, ending with a Rnd 1 or 3.

Divide back & front
Maintaining established pat, beg with Row 2 or Row 4 (RS), bind off 2 (4, 4, 4, 5) sts, work in pat to marker and turn, leaving rem sts on spare needle or holder. Bind off 2 (4, 4, 4, 5), and then purl across back sts.

Back
Continue to work established pat in rows, dec 1 st at each edge [every RS row] 13 (18, 20, 23, 23) times—66 (68, 72, 74, 80) sts.

Work even until armhole measures 6¾ (7, 7½, 7¾, 8¼) inches, ending with a WS row.

Shape neck & shoulders
Work across 20 sts, join 2nd skein of yarn, bind off 26 (28, 32, 34, 40) sts, work to end. Working both sides at once with separate skeins of yarn, dec 1 st at each neck edge [every row] 4 (4, 4, 3, 2) times. Place rem 16 (16, 16, 17, 18) shoulder sts on holders.

Left Front
With RS facing and maintaining established pat, join yarn, bind off 2 (4, 4, 4, 5) sts, work 46 (52, 56, 60, 63) sts for left front (including st rem from bind-off), turn, leaving rem sts on needle or holder. Purl across.

Working on left front only, dec 1 st at armhole edge [every RS row] 13 (18, 20, 23, 23) times, and *at the same time*, dec 1 st at neck edge [every 3 rows] 17 (18, 20, 20, 22) times—16 (16, 16, 17, 18) sts.

Work even until armhole measures same as back to shoulder. Place rem sts on holder.

Right Front
With RS facing and maintaining pat, join yarn and work to end of row, turn. At beg of next row (WS), bind off 2 (4, 4, 4, 5) sts; purl across.

Dec 1 st at armhole edge [every RS row] 13 (18, 20, 23, 23) times, and *at the same time*, dec 1 st at neck edge [every 3 rows] 17 (18, 20, 20, 22) times—16 (16, 17, 18) sts.

Work even until front measures same as back to shoulder. Place rem sts on holder.

Assembly
Bind off front and back shoulders using 3-needle bind-off, page 122.

Armbands
With 16-inch circular needle and with RS facing, pick up and knit 76 (80, 86, 92, 98) sts around armhole. Work 5 rnds in St st. Bind off loosely.

Rep for 2nd armhole.

Neckband
Beg at right shoulder seam and with RS facing, pick up and knit 36 (38, 40, 44, 48) sts across back neck, 40 (42, 44, 46, 49) sts along left front neck edge, 40 (42, 44, 46, 49) sts along right front neck edge— 116 (122, 128, 136, 146) sts.

Work 5 rnds in St st. Bind off loosely.

Block to size, allowing St st edges to roll naturally. ●

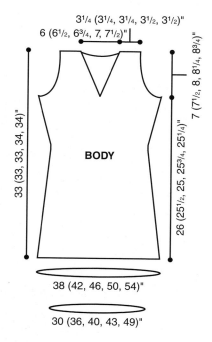

3¼ (3¼, 3¼, 3½, 3½)"

6 (6½, 6¾, 7, 7½)"

7 (7½, 8, 8¼, 8¾)"

33 (33, 33, 34, 34)"

26 (25½, 25, 25¾, 25¼)"

BODY

38 (42, 46, 50, 54)"

30 (36, 40, 43, 49)"

Paneled Lace Afghan

Use one color per panel, or make it in one hue—you'll love this throw!

Design by JoAnne Turcotte for Plymouth Yarn Co.

Skill Level

■■■□ INTERMEDIATE

Finished Size
Approx 47 x 53 inches

Materials
- Plymouth Yarn Fantasy Naturale (worsted weight: 100% mercerized cotton; 140 yds/100g per skein): 3 skeins each blue #2574 (A), lemon #1242 (B), aqua #8012 (C), pink #6188 (D) and lavender #6399 (E); 1 skein white #8001 (F)

  4 MEDIUM
- Size 6 (4mm) needles
- Size 7 (4.5mm) needles or size needed to obtain gauge
- Cable needle
- Size G/6 (4mm) crochet hook

Gauge
18 sts = 4 inches/10cm in pat with larger needles.

To save time, take time to check gauge.

Special Abbreviations
Back Cross (BC): Slip 4 sts to cn, hold in back, k4, k4 from cn.

Front Cross (FC): Slip 4 sts to cn, hold in front, k4, k4 from cn.

Pattern Note
Make 1 strip with each color indicated; each strip should be approximately 9 inches wide.

Panel
Make 1 each A, B, C, D & E

With smaller needles, loosely cast on 40 sts.

Knit 8 rows. Change to larger needles.

Beg pat
Row 1 (RS): K4, p1, k8, p1, k2tog, k2, yo, k1, yo, k5, ssk, p1, k8, p1, k4.

Row 2 and all WS rows: K4, k1, p8, k1, p12, k1, p8, k1, k4.

Row 3: K4, p1, k8, p1, k2tog, k1, yo, k3, yo, k4, ssk, p1, k8, p1, k4.

Row 5: K4, p1, BC, p1, k2tog, yo, k5, yo, k3, ssk, p1, FC, p1, k4.

Row 7: K4, p1, k8, p1, k2tog, k5, yo, k1, yo, k2, ssk, p1, k8, p1, k4.

Row 9: K4, p1, k8, p1, k2tog, k4, yo, k3, yo, k1, ssk, p1, k8, p1, k4.

Row 11: K4, p1, k8, p1, k2tog, k3, yo, k5, yo, ssk, p1, k8, p1, k4.

Row 12: K4, k1, p8, k1, p12, k1, p8, k1, k4.

Rep Rows 1–12 until strip measures approx 52 inches, ending with a Row 8.

***Note:** In photographed afghan, cables were crossed 26 times.*

Change to smaller needles.

Knit 8 rows. Bind off loosely.

Assembly
Sew strips tog in following order: A, B, C, D and E.

Border
***Note:** If not familiar with reverse single crochet st (reverse sc), see page 122.*

Beg at lower LH corner, with RS facing, crochet hook and F, work from left to right along side edge as follows: reverse sc, [ch 1, skip 1 ridge, reverse sc in next ridge] to top corner, work corner as: [reverse sc, ch 1, work reverse sc], *ch 1, skip 2 sts, reverse sc; rep from * across top edge to next corner, work corner as before, [ch 1, skip 1 ridge, reverse sc in next ridge] to bottom corner, work corner as before, work across bottom edge as for top edge. Sl st to first st. Fasten off. ●

Little Miss Precious

Here's a dressy poncho for a young, sugar 'n' spice girl. Change the ribbon for everyday wear!

Design by Julie Gaddy

Skill Level

◼◼◼◻ INTERMEDIATE

Finished Measurements
Circumference at lower edge: Approx 42 inches
Length: 7½ inches

Materials
- Worsted weight yarn (100% wool; 80 yds/50g per skein): 3 skeins pink
- Size 5 (3.75mm) 16-inch circular needle
- Size 8 (5mm) 24-inch circular needle or size needed to obtain gauge
- Stitch markers, 1 in CC for beg of rnd
- Approx 3½ yds ribbon

Gauge
18 sts and 24 rows = 4 inches/10cm in St st with larger needles.

To save time, take time to check gauge.

Special Abbreviations
Make 1 Right (M1R): Insert LH needle from back to front under strand between the last st worked and the next st on LH needle, k1 through front of loop. St slants to the right.

Make 1 Left (M1L): Insert LH needle from front to back under strand between the last st worked and the next st on LH needle, k1-tbl. St slants to the left.

Body

Neckband
With smaller needle, cast on 80 sts. Place marker for beg of rnd and join without twisting.

Rnds 1–3: Knit around.

Rnd 4 (eyelet rnd): *K3, yo, k2tog; rep from * around.

Rnds 5 and 6: Knit around.

Rnd 7 (turning ridge): Purl around.

Rnds 8 and 9: Knit around.

Rnd 10 (eyelet rnd): Rep Rnd 4.

Rnds 11–13: Knit around.

Beg raglan shaping
Change to larger circular needle and knit 1 rnd, placing markers for raglan shaping as follows: K13, place marker, k14, place marker, k26, place marker, k14, place marker, k13, leave beg of marker in place.

Rnd 1 (Inc rnd): *Knit to 1 st before raglan marker, M1R, k1, sl marker, k1, M1L; rep from * around (8 sts inc)—88 sts.

Rnd 2: Knit around.

Rep [Rnds 1 and 2] 8 times more—152 sts.

Work even in St st (knit every rnd) until poncho measures 3 inches from last inc rnd or ½ inch less than desired length.

Eyelet Border
Rnd 1: *K1, p1; rep from * around.

Rnd 2 (eyelet rnd): *[P1, k1] twice, yo, k2tog; rep from * until 14 sts rem, end [p1, k1] twice, p1, yo, p2tog, [k1, p1] twice, k1, yo, k2tog.

Beg with a knit st, bind off all sts in seed st (purl the knit sts and knit the purl sts).

Finishing
Fold neckband to inside along turning ridge. Match eyelets on inside of neckband to eyelets on outside of neckband, neatly sew neckband facing inside of poncho. Use a loose tension on sewing yarn so neckband will retain its stretch.

Block as desired.

Referring to photo, beg off-center and weave ribbon in and out of eyelets in neckband. Tie bow and trim ribbon ends.

Rep along bottom edge. ●

Winter Warmth Hat & Mittens

A snuggly hat and matching mittens are great gift items.

Designs by Diane Zangl

Skill Level

■■■□ INTERMEDIATE

Sizes

Hat: 1 size fits most
Mittens: Woman's small/medium (medium/large) Instructions are given for smaller size, with larger size in parentheses. When only 1 number is given, it applies to both sizes.

Finished Measurements

Hand circumference: 7½ (9) inches
Length: 9 (10) inches

Materials

- Artful Yarns Circus (super chunky weight; 95% wool/5% acrylic; 93 yds/100g per ball): 2 balls side show #10 (MC) **[6 SUPER BULKY]**
- Artful Yarns Portrait (bulky weight; 70% mohair/25% viscose/5% polyester; 164 yds/50g per ball): 1 ball Fazio's mistress #114 (CC) **[5 BULKY]**
- Size 9 (5.5mm) 16-inch circular and set of 5 double-point needles or size needed to obtain gauge
- Stitch markers
- Stitch holders
- 2 (6-inch strands) of smooth, contrasting-color scrap yarn

Gauge

10 sts and 16 rows = 4 inches/10cm in rev St st with MC.

To save time, take time to check gauge.

Special Abbreviation

Make 1 (M1): Make backward loop on RH needle.

Pattern Notes

Yarn amounts are sufficient to make hat and mittens.

Two strands of CC yarn are held together throughout cuffs.

Hat

With MC and circular needle, cast on 52 sts. Place marker on needle and join without twisting. Work even in rev St st until hat measures 7 inches from beg, dec 3 sts evenly on last rnd—49 sts.

Place marker after every 7th st.

Shape crown

Dec rnd: [Purl to 2 sts before marker, p2tog] 7 times—7 sts dec.

Work 1 rnd even.

Rep last 2 rnds until 7 sts rem, changing to dpns when necessary. Cut yarn, leaving a long end. Weave end through rem sts and pull up tightly.

Cuff

With circular needle and 2 strands of CC held tog, WS facing, pick up and knit 1 st in each cast-on st at lower edge—52 sts.

Place marker on needle and join to work in rnds.

Inc rnd: *K4, M1; rep from * around—65 sts.

Work even in garter st (purl 1 rnd, knit 1 rnd) until cuff measures 2 inches above picked-up row. Bind off all sts.

Turn cuff up over body of hat. Tack in place, if desired.

Mittens
Make 2 alike

Hand

With MC and dpns, cast on 20 (24) sts, divide onto 4 needles. Place marker on needle and join without twisting.

Work even in rev St st until mitten measures 4 (4½) inches.

Mark for thumb

Next rnd: P2, drop working yarn. With scrap yarn, k3 and place sts just worked back on LH needle. Pick up working yarn and purl these 3 sts, work to end of rnd.

Work even until mitten measures 8 (9) inches from beg. Place marker after every 5th (6th) st.

Shape top

Dec rnd: [Purl to 2 sts before marker, p2tog] 4 times—4 sts dec.

Work 1 rnd even.

Rep last 2 rnds until 5 (6) sts rem.

Cut yarn, leaving a long end. Weave end through rem sts and pull up tightly.

Thumb

Pick out CC scrap yarn and place resulting 7 loops on 3 needles: 2 sts on each of 2 needles closest to top of hand, 3 sts on lower needle. With top needles, pick up 1 strand on each end of opening—9 sts; 3 on each needle.

Join yarn at beg of left top needle. Work even in rev St st for 2½ (3) inches.

Shape top

Rnd 1: [P1, p2tog] 3 times—6 sts.

Rnd 2: Purl around.

Rnd 3: [P2tog] around—3 sts.

Cut yarn, leaving a long end. Weave end through rem sts and pull up tightly.

Cuff

With WS facing, using dpn and 2 strands of CC held tog, pick up and knit 1 st in each cast-on st at lower edge—20 (24) sts.

Place marker on needle and join to work in rnds.

Inc rnd: *K4, M1; rep from * around—25 (30) sts.

Work even in garter st until cuff measures 1½ inches above picked-up row. Bind off all sts.

Turn cuff up over mitten body.

Tack in place, if desired. Press thumbs to opposite sides for right and left mittens. ●

General Information

Standard Abbreviations

[ ] work instructions within brackets as many times as directed
( ) work instructions within parentheses in the place directed
** repeat instructions following the asterisks as directed
* repeat instructions following the single asterisk as directed
" inch(es)

approx approximately
beg begin/begins/beginning
CC contrasting color
ch chain stitch
cm centimeter(s)
cn cable needle
dec decrease/decreases/decreasing
dpn(s) double-point needle(s)
g gram(s)
inc increase/increases/increasing
k knit

k2tog knit 2 stitches together
kwise knitwise
LH left hand
m meter(s)
M1 make one stitch
MC main color
mm millimeter(s)
oz ounce(s)
p purl
pat(s) pattern(s)
p2tog purl 2 stitches together
psso pass slipped stitch over
pwise purlwise
rem remain/remains/remaining
rep repeat(s)
rev St st reverse stockinette stitch
RH right hand
rnd(s) rounds
RS right side
skp slip, knit, pass slipped stitch over—1 stitch decreased

sk2p slip 1, knit 2 together, pass slipped stitch over the knit 2 together—2 stitches decreased
sl slip
sl 1kwise slip 1 knitwise
sl 1pwise slip 1 purlwise
sl st slip stitch(es)
ssk slip, slip, knit these 2 stitches together—a decrease
st(s) stitch(es)
St st stockinette stitch
tbl through back loop(s)
tog together
WS wrong side
wyib with yarn in back
wyif with yarn in front
yd(s) yard(s)
yfwd yarn forward
yo (yo's) yarn over(s)

Standard Yarn Weight System
Categories of yarn, gauge ranges, and recommended needle sizes

Yarn Weight Symbol & Category Names	0 LACE	1 SUPER FINE	2 FINE	3 LIGHT	4 MEDIUM	5 BULKY	6 SUPER BULKY
Type of Yarns in Category	Fingering 10-Count Crochet Thread	Sock, Fingering, Baby	Sport, Baby	DK, Light Worsted	Worsted, Afghan, Aran	Chunky, Craft, Rug	Bulky, Roving
Knit Gauge Range* in Stockinette Stitch to 4 inches	33–40 sts**	27–32 sts	23–26 sts	21–24 sts	16–20 sts	12–15 sts	6–11 sts
Recommended Needle in Metric Size Range	1.5–2.25mm	2.25–3.25mm	3.25–3.75mm	3.75–4.5mm	4.5–5.5mm	5.5–8mm	8mm and larger
Recommended Needle U.S. Size Range	000 to 1	1 to 3	3 to 5	5 to 7	7 to 9	9 to 11	11 and larger

* GUIDELINES ONLY: The above reflect the most commonly used gauges and needle sizes for specific yarn categories.

** Lace weight yarns are usually knitted on larger needles and hooks to create lacy, openwork patterns. Accordingly, a gauge range is difficult to determine. Always follow the gauge stated in your pattern.

Knitting Needle Conversion Chart

U.S.	1	2	3	4	5	6	7	8	9	10	10½	11	13	15	17	19	35	50
Continental-mm	2.25	2.75	3.25	3.5	3.75	4	4.5	5	5.5	6	6.5	8	9	10	12.75	15	19	25

Inches Into Millimeters & Centimeters
All measurements are rounded off slightly.

inches	mm	cm	inches	cm	inches	cm	inches	cm
⅛	3	0.3	5	12.5	21	53.5	38	96.5
¼	6	0.6	5½	14	22	56.0	39	99.0
⅜	10	1.0	6	15.0	23	58.5	40	101.5
½	13	1.3	7	18.0	24	61.0	41	104.0
⅝	15	1.5	8	20.5	25	63.5	42	106.5
¾	20	2.0	9	23.0	26	66.0	43	109.0
⅞	22	2.2	10	25.5	27	68.5	44	112.0
1	25	2.5	11	28.0	28	71.0	45	114.5
1¼	32	3.2	12	30.5	29	73.5	46	117.0
1½	38	3.8	13	33.0	30	76.0	47	119.5
1¾	45	4.5	14	35.5	31	79.0	48	122.0
2	50	5.0	15	38.0	32	81.5	49	124.5
2½	65	6.5	16	40.5	33	84.0	50	127.0
3	75	7.5	17	43.0	34	86.5		
3½	90	9.0	18	46.0	35	89.0		
4	100	10.0	19	48.5	36	91.5		
4½	115	11.5	20	51.0	37	94.0		

Skill Levels

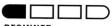

BEGINNER

Beginner projects for first-time knitters using basic stitches. Minimal shaping.

EASY

Easy projects using basic stitches, repetitive stitch patterns, simple color changes and simple shaping and finishing.

INTERMEDIATE

Intermediate projects with a variety of stitches, mid-level shaping and finishing.

EXPERIENCED

Experienced projects using advanced techniques and stitches, detailed shaping and refined finishing.

Knitting Basics

Cast-On

Leaving an end about an inch long for each stitch to be cast on, make a slip knot on the right needle.

Place the thumb and index finger of your left hand between the yarn ends with the long yarn end over your thumb, and the strand from the skein over your index finger. Close your other fingers over the strands to hold them against your palm. Spread your thumb and index fingers apart and draw the yarn into a "V."

Place the needle in front of the strand around your thumb and bring it underneath this strand. Carry the needle over and under the strand on your index finger.

Draw through loop on thumb.

Drop the loop from your thumb and draw up the strand to form a stitch on the needle.

Repeat until you have cast on the number of stitches indicated in the pattern. Remember to count the beginning slip knot as a stitch.

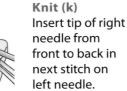

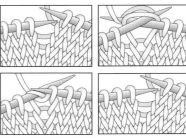

Cable Cast-On

This type of cast-on is used when adding stitches in the middle or at the end of a row.

Make a slip knot on the left needle. Knit a stitch in this knot and place it on the left needle. Insert the right needle between the last two stitches on the left needle. Knit a stitch and place it on the left needle. Repeat for each stitch needed.

Knit (k)

Insert tip of right needle from front to back in next stitch on left needle.

Bring yarn under and over the tip of the right needle.

Pull yarn loop through the stitch with right needle point.

Slide the stitch off the left needle. The new stitch is on the right needle.

Purl (p)

With yarn in front, insert tip of right needle from back to front through next stitch on the left needle.

Bring yarn around the right needle counterclockwise.

With right needle, draw yarn back through the stitch.

Slide the stitch off the left needle. The new stitch is on the right needle.

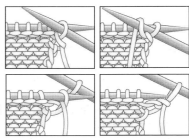

Bind-Off

Binding off (knit)

Knit first two stitches on left needle. Insert tip of left needle into first stitch worked on right needle and pull it over the second stitch and completely off the needle.

Knit the next stitch and repeat. When one stitch remains on right needle, cut yarn and draw tail through last stitch to fasten off.

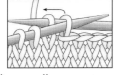

Binding off (purl)

Purl first two stitches on left needle. Insert tip of left needle into first stitch worked on right needle and pull it over the second stitch and completely off the needle.

Purl the next stitch and repeat. When one stitch remains on right needle, cut yarn and draw tail through last stitch to fasten off.

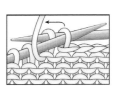

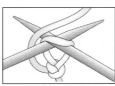
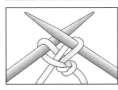

Increase (inc)

Two stitches in one stitch

Increase (knit)

Knit the next stitch in the usual manner, but don't remove the stitch from the left needle. Place right needle behind left needle and knit again into the back of the same stitch. Slip original stitch off left needle.

Increase (purl)

Purl the next stitch in the usual manner, but don't remove the stitch from the left needle. Place right needle behind left needle and purl again into the back of the same stitch. Slip original stitch off left needle.

Invisible Increase (M1)

There are several ways to make or increase one stitch.

Make 1 with Left Twist (M1L)

Insert left needle from front to back under the horizontal loop between the last stitch worked and next stitch on left needle.

With right needle, knit into the back of this loop.

To make this increase on the purl side, insert left needle in same manner and purl into the back of the loop.

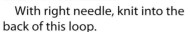

Make 1 with Right Twist (M1R)

Insert left needle from back to front under the horizontal loop between the last stitch worked and next stitch on left needle.

With right needle, knit into the front of this loop.

To make this increase on the purl side, insert left needle in same manner and purl into the front of the loop.

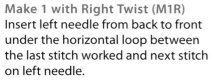

Make 1 with Backward Loop over the right needle

With your thumb, make a loop over the right needle.

Slip the loop from your thumb onto the needle and pull to tighten.

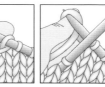

Make 1 in top of stitch below

Insert tip of right needle into the stitch on left needle one row below.

Knit this stitch, then knit the stitch on the left needle.

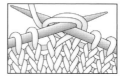

Decrease (dec)

Knit 2 together (k2tog)

Put tip of right needle through next two stitches on left needle as to knit. Knit these two stitches as one.

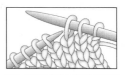

Purl 2 together (p2tog)

Put tip of right needle through next two stitches on left needle as to purl. Purl these two stitches as one.

Slip, Slip, Knit (ssk)

Slip next two stitches, one at a time, as to knit from left needle to right needle.

Insert left needle in front of both stitches and work off needle together.

Slip, Slip, Purl (ssp)

Slip next two stitches, one at a time, as to knit from left needle to right needle. Slip these stitches back onto left needle keeping them twisted. Purl these two stitches together through back loops.

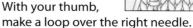

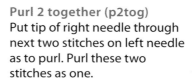

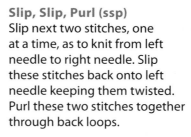

Kitchener Stitch

This method of weaving with two needles is used for the toes of socks and flat seams. To weave the edges together and form an unbroken line of stockinette stitch, divide all stitches evenly onto two knitting needles—one behind the other. Thread yarn into tapestry needle. Hold needles with wrong sides together and work from right to left as follows:

Step 1:
Insert tapestry needle into first stitch on front needle as to purl. Draw yarn through stitch, leaving stitch on knitting needle.

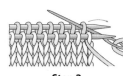

Step 1

Step 2:
Insert tapestry needle into the first stitch on the back needle as to purl. Draw yarn through stitch and slip stitch off knitting needle.

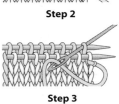

Step 2

Step 3:
Insert tapestry needle into the next stitch on same (back) needle as to knit, leaving stitch on knitting needle.

Step 3

Step 4:
Insert tapestry needle into the first stitch on the front needle as to knit. Draw yarn through stitch and slip stitch off knitting needle.

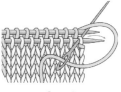

Step 4

Step 5:
Insert tapestry needle into the next stitch on same (front) needle as to purl. Draw yarn through stitch, leaving stitch on knitting needle.

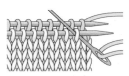

Step 5

Repeat Steps 2–5 until one stitch is left on each needle. Then repeat Steps 2 and 4. Fasten off. Woven stitches should be the same size as adjacent knitted stitches.

3-Needle Bind-Off

Use this technique for seaming two edges together, such as when joining a shoulder seam. Hold the edge stitches on two separate needles with right sides together.

With a third needle, knit together a stitch from the front needle with one from the back.

Repeat, knitting a stitch from the front needle with one from the back needle once more.

Slip the first stitch over the second.

Repeat knitting, a front and back pair of stitches together, then bind one off.

Crochet Stitches

Chain Stitch

Slip Stitch

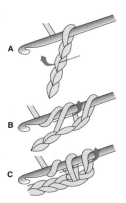

Single Crochet

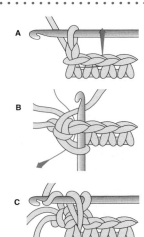

Reverse Single Crochet

Fringe & Tassels

Single-Knot Fringe

Step 1: Cut equal lengths of yarn twice the length of the desired finished fringe.

Step 2: Insert a crochet hook from front to back into the last row or edge of finished work. Fold cut yarn in half and pull center of fold through to front.

Step 3: Take both ends and bring them through the loop; pull tightly, referring to Photo 1.

Repeat across the entire edge evenly to complete the fringe as shown in Photo 2.

Trim even.

Photo 1

Photo 2

Single Tassel

Step 1: Wrap yarn around a piece of cardboard the length of desired finished tassel.

Step 2: Thread a yarn needle with 12 inches of the same yarn and thread behind the loops on one side near the top. Tie that yarn tightly around the loops on the top edge. Cut across the bottom edge to make a bunch of strands that is gathered in the center as in Photo 3.

Step 3: Make a slip knot and slide it over the top of the folded tassel. Tie tightly and continue to wind around the tassel as desired. Cut the yarn and thread it back onto the needle. Insert the needle through the wraps and pull tightly out through the bottom. Cut to the length of other tassel fringes.

Step 4: Use the top tails to tie and secure to fabric, as shown in Photo 4; the completed edge is shown in Photo 5.

Photo 3

Photo 4

Photo 5

Embroidery

Embroidery accents add a special touch to any knitted item. Embroidery stitches can be used with various yarns in either symmetrical or random patterns. Because knitted stitches are looser than woven fabric, it's best to use an appropriate weight of contrasting yarn to show off the embroidery to its fullest. Use a blunt tapestry needle with a big eye for stitching. In all cases, avoid making knots on the back of the work; weave in the tail rather than creating a knot to start your work.

Single Chain Stitch

Step 1: Bring the threaded needle from the back of the work to the front. Slide the needle back through the same hole and out through the front of the fabric about an ⅛ inch away, catching a loop under the needle.

Step 2: Pull the needle through without tightening the loop. The working yarn will be on the inside of the loop.

Step 3: Insert the needle from front to back just on the outside of the yarn to anchor the loop, as presented in Photo 1.

Photo 1

Running Chain Stitch

Step 1: Bring the threaded needle to the front of the work. In one move, slide the needle back through the same hole and out through the front of the fabric about ⅛ inch away, catching a loop under the needle.

Step 2: Pull the needle through without tightening the loop. The working yarn will be on the inside of the loop.

Referring to Photo 2, repeat Steps 1 and 2 to desired length of chain.

Photo 2

Feather Stitch

Step 1: Bring the threaded needle to the front of the work at the top of where the feather chain will begin.

Step 2: In one move, slide the needle through the knitting ⅛ inch to the right and bring it back out ⅛ inch below, directly between the two points, catching the working yarn under the needle.

Step 3: Pull the needle through without tightening too much.

Refer to Photo 3, and continue Steps 2 and 3 either to the right or to the left as desired.

Photo 3

Beaded Embroidery

Step 1: After creating a running chain, straight stitch two lines at the bottom of each chain through the same hole, as shown in Photo 4.

Step 2: Sew beads at the ends of the lines with upholstery thread that matches the main fabric to accent as desired, as shown in Photo 5.

Photo 4

Photo 5

Blanket Stitch

The blanket stitch is a wonderful finish to cuff, collar and hem edges.

Step 1: Working left to right at the edge of your piece, bring the threaded needle to the front of the work.

Step 2: In one move, insert the needle ¼ inch above and ⅛ inch to the right and back out even with the original point, catching the working yarn under the needle, as shown in Photo 6.

Step 3: Pull the needle through, tightening the right angle created.

Referring to Photos 6 and 7, repeat Steps 2 and 3 evenly across the edge. Photo 8 shows the completed Blanket Stitch edge. The length and width between stitches can vary as desired.

Photo 6

Photo 7

Photo 8

French Knot

Step 1: Bring the threaded needle to the front of the work.

Step 2: With the point of the needle facing down, wind the yarn around the needle clockwise two times.

Step 3: Bring the working yarn under the needle, catching the yarn to lock the stitch in place. Slide the knot to the fabric and insert the needle back into the fabric on the other side of the same stitch where you began.

Step 4: Holding the knot on the front of the fabric, take the needle through the knot and pull excess yarn to the back of the fabric as shown in Photo 9.

Photo 9

Straight Stitch/Satin Stitch

Step 1: Bring the threaded needle to the front of the work.

Step 2: In one move, insert needle ⅛–¼ inch away.

For the satin stitch, continue to do straight stitches next to each other to fill in a desired shape as shown in Photo 10.

Photo 10

Combining Embroidery Stitches

Any of these stitches can be combined in a free-style method to create gorgeous floral accents, as illustrated in Photo 11. Start with the branches and leaves, and build the flowers over them.

Photo 11

Duplicate Stitch

The duplicate stitch is an embroidery stitch that mimics the actual knitted stitches of a finished piece to add color and pattern to the surface.

Avoid knots on the wrong side of your work by weaving in the tail.

Step 1: Bring the threaded needle to the front of the work at the bottom V of a knit stitch.

Step 2: Follow the path of that stitch by inserting the needle through the 2 legs of the stitch above.

Step 3: Insert the needle back through the original point.

Continue to repeat Steps 1 and 2, referring to Photos 12 and 13, in any direction you like, always following the path of the knitted stitches.

Photo 12

Photo 13

Photo Index

8

13

10

15

17

19

20

22

25

26

28

31

33

34

37

38

40

42

45

46

49

50

52

55

56

60

62

64

67

70

72

75

79

81

85

86

89

90

93

95

98

101

103

106

109

113

114

116